A MASS FOR JESSE JAMES

By the same author:

THE POLITICS OF MAGIC
The work and times of Tom Murphy

NO MORE HEROES
A radical guide to Shakespeare

THE SOUTHERN QUESTION

(all published by Raven Arts Press)

Also available as a companion piece to this title:

THE TRAIL OF THE GENERALS
Selected journalism 1980-1990
Colm Toibin

"A MASS FOR JESSE JAMES

A JOURNEY THROUGH 1980'S IRELAND"

FINTAN O'TOOLE

A MASS FOR JESSE JAMES is first
published in 1990 by
The Raven Arts Press
P.O.Box 1430
Finglas
Dublin 11
Ireland

ISBN 1 85186 078 9

DA
959.1
.086
1990
Cop.1

Designed by Dermot Bolger and Aidan Murphy. Cover design by
Rapid Productions. Cover photograph by *The Irish Times*. Printed and
bound in Ireland by Colour Books Ltd., Baldoyle. Special thanks to
Gillian Doran.

CONTENTS

For Samuel and Fionn

INTRODUCTION
Ireland in the Eighties

Towards the end of the 1980s, an architect in the Office of Public Works in Dublin, the body responsible for state buildings, was given a job to do, the job of designing a new customs post for the border that divides the two Irelands, North and South. The old post was a glorified shed. The customs men and women had to stand out in the rain that falls most of the time, while they checked the trucks and cars going through for the hidden tanks of petrol or the covert televisions out of which nationalists on both sides made their living. They had been complaining for years about their conditions of work, waiting in lobbies, lobbying in waiting rooms, putting their cases to the private secretaries of junior ministers. But government was there to solve all problems, eventually, and at last its machinery moved.

The architect was conscientious and careful. He talked to the customs officers about their working lives and how they could be improved. He looked at the site and at the way that lorries and cars would come through it. And he went back to Dublin and designed a fine, solid building, with a sloping glass canopy which the vehicles could drive under, protecting the officers and drivers from the rain. And then he sent his plans up the line to be approved.

Approval was a formality. No one in the bureaucracy was much interested in aesthetics. Drawings were hardly ever looked at in detail, only the bottom line that showed the cost to be within budget. But not this time. This time the message came down with stunning speed and unheard-of sureness. This building was under no circumstances to be constructed. It was, the word had it, too solid, too comfortable, too grand altogether. It was too *permanent* looking. And since state policy held that the border itself was temporary, an aberration, a white line chalked across the country that would disappear in the hard rain of history, it followed that border posts must be ramshackle, half-built, temporary. And so the architect built a border post that looked pretty much like the old one. And the workers continued to stand out in the rain.

The 1980s wer   became

absolute, when the attempt to construct a realm of symbols and images and values that would be unchanging came into ever sharper conflict with a shifting, divided and contradictory reality. If such a decade can have heroes, then the heroes of 1980s Ireland were Tom Flynn, Noel Murray and Keith Byrne. For two weeks at the beginning of 1985, at the most painfully revelatory public event of the decade, the Kerry Babies Tribunal, a judical inquiry into how a young Kerry woman had come to confess to the murder of a new-born child that could not possibly have been hers, the name of Tom Flynn dominated the proceedings and held the nation spellbound. His name had been found written in blue biro on a mattress taken from the young woman's house. He became famous, a national figure, because no one knew who he was. Six weeks later, it was revealed that he had worked in the furniture shop where the mattress was bought, that he had nothing whatsoever to do with the case, and that he was now in America. He was the 1980s Irish version of Kilroy, the man caught up in big events swirling around his head, the absurd actor wandering into a plot that is not of his devising, except that in his case he was the man who wasn't there, the man who, like more and more young Irish people as the 1980s went on, chose to emigrate, to be elsewhere.

Noel Murray and Keith Byrne were two Dublin boys, both under 13, who went missing and then turned up a few days later in New York. They had stowed away on a ferry to England, then stowed away on a jumbo jet from Heathrow to JFK Airport in New York. When asked how this had happened, the security staff at Heathrow said that it did not happen. It was impossible. What may not be could not be. Tom Flynn, being absent, was at his most real. The two boys, being real, had to be made absent, impossible. All three ended up in America. Such were the convoluted and perverse relationships between image and reality, between absence and presence, which faced Irish society in the 1980s. In a world that is officially impermanent, opposites cannot hold their places and continually melt into each other.

Real life becomes as surreal as avant-garde art. How for example, can a sculptor compete with moving statues? In 1985 and 1986, Ireland was swept by a wave of devotion as statues of the Blessed Virgin in remote churches and grottos were seen to move, waving, weeping, floating. Huge crowds gathered to witness the manifestations which stopped only when the rains of winter began, making it less pleasant for the crowds to gather in the open air.

How can a writer compete with a name scrawled in blue biro on an infamous mattress, or with the impassioned public debates about the forms and meanings of words which surrounded the insertion of a clause prohibiting abortion in the Irish Constitution in 1983? How can a painter compete with the eloquence of excrement smeared on the walls of their cells by IRA prisoners in the H-Blocks in Northern Ireland in a "dirty protest" that dominated the national psyche in 1981 and 1982? The problem of Irish culture in the 1980s is not the problem of the way in which reality is to be aesthetically represented. It is the problem of dealing with a reality that is itself deeply aesthetic, inextricably bound up with the symbolic, the imaginary, the metaphorical.

For Ireland, the 1980s began in 1979 and ended in 1989. They are bounded by the Second Oil Crisis on the one side and the upheavals of Europe on the other, the end of one dream and the beginning of some kind of often fearful awakening. The tilting over into recession of the world economy in 1979 finally brought an end to the Irish dream of the 1960s, the dream that someone else could do our developing for us, that the policy that got underway in the late 1950s of doing everything possible to attract foreign multinational investment would of itself solve our problems. In the 1980s, that dream became a nightmare as foreign investment became foreign debt, as inflows turned into outflows — of money, people and energies. And by 1989, as the crawl towards European integration became a rush, the idea of "Ireland" itself had become deeply problematic. Something new had started and no one was sure what it was, what place, if any, this place would continue to have.

The 1980s then, was a time of slow crisis, of creeping catastrophe, of petty apocalypse. The national debt rose to well in excess of £20 billion. Unemployment rose to a quarter of a million. A further quarter of a million, out of a population of only 3.5 million, left the country during the 1980s. By the end of the decade, a third of the population was living below the poverty line. In 1989, for the first time since the miracle years of the 1960s the population of what had regarded itself as the fastest-growing country of the western world, actually declined, so that in 1989 it was no higher than it had been in 1889 after four decades of famine, strife and mass emigration to the New World.

By the middle of the eighties, the common currency of political debate was of the country going under, of the IMF being at the door, of the international bankers to whom we owed our existence getting ready to foreclose on Ireland Inc. The return of mass emigration, most of it among young people, added to the sense of an endgame,

9

of the lack of a future. Looking at the massive outflows of capital and profits from the country, about 8 per cent of Gross Domestic Product a year, the economists started talking of the Black Hole and the image stuck, seeming to sum up the sense of a place that was imploding under the weight of collapsed dreams.

But day to day, this was the most mundane apocalypse imaginable. It was made up of the tedium of dole queues, the frustration of hospital queues, the half-demented expectation of queues at the American Embassy in Dublin for temporary visas that would become, when the visas expired, passports to an underground existence as an "undocumented alien" in Boston or the Bronx or the new Irish colony of Queens. And, meanwhile, nothing actually collapsed, nothing came to a halt. The immediate crisis in the public finances was tackled in the last third of the decade and the IMF faded out of the picture. Something mysterious called "confidence" returned, a huge new Financial Services Centre, a Cayman Islands in the middle of Dublin city, was built, property prices boomed. The queues went on, but by now we were so used to them that we stopped seeing them. A new Hidden Ireland came into being, an Ireland of undocumented aliens in their own country, invisible, unheard, with no official culture, no place in the sun. Their visas had expired, their permits were up, their deadlines had passed. But they still hadn't got to the top of the queue.

And so, in the eighties, Ireland became both known and unknowable. On the one hand, a country which had hysterically guarded its intimate secrets turned these secrets into a public show. In the H-Block campaigns in the North, excrement became a weapon of war. In the abortion referendum of 1983, wombs, periods, sperms and eggs, unpious ejaculations and ectopic pregnancies became the terms of political debate. In the Kerry Babies inquiry, the possibilities of fertilisation, the mechanics of giving birth, the look of blood on the bedclothes, the possibility that a woman might have sexual intercourse with two different men on the same day and conceive twins who would have different fathers, filled minds, hearts and column inches for eight months. On the streets and country lanes of Northern Ireland, intimate human blood flowed and was seen in living colour on the tv screens. In the divorce referendum (on whether or not to remove the stipulation in the Irish Constitution that prohibits divorce), the intimate cruelties and pleasures of marriage were discussed in the way that the current budget deficit or the unemployment figures might be discussed. Around this time, a government junior minister, meaning to say

10

"fiscal rectitude" (the catch-cry of the time), said "physical rectitude" instead. At no time and in no country can there ever have been so much body in the body politic, can the functions of the human body have formed so great a part of the public realm.

But the more things became known, the more privacies were exposed and revealed, the more unknowable the country became. Between the resurgence of Irish nationalism at the end of the nineteenth century and the social transformation of the 1960s, "Ireland" was a single, imaginable entity. The dominant cultural and political orthodoxy, Gaelic, Catholic and nationalist, was very dominant indeed. Those who were not a part of it — urban workers, Northern Protestants, the streams of emigrants that flowed unabated to England and America, women who did not hold to their Constitutional position of a "life within the home" - never saw themselves as having anything in common with each other and could therefore be ignored or dismissed or deferred. The official image of the culture was that it was rural, classless and anti-materialist, and even the most sophisticated of the artists tended not to challenge this assumption.

Slowly but inexorably, through the sixties and seventies, those assumptions became untenable. And, more importantly still, the assumptions which had been replacing them — the image of Ireland put forward in the Industrial Development Authority's ads in "Time" magazine: "The most profitable location in Europe for US industry" — also began to fall apart in the eighties. The first tenet of Irish nationalism, which had sustained Irish politics for a century, was that differences between Irish people were unimportant when compared with their common culture and interests. In the eighties, the differences were unavoidable. In the North, they were the ferocious differences of a tribal war. In the South, they were the growing tensions between urban and rural (with the urban population now for a first time a majority), between haves and have nots, and between an increasingly vocal secularised liberal minority and an increasingly entrenched and embattled traditional Catholic majority.

These divisions intermingled and clashed. In the referenda on divorce and abortion, both won with a 2-1 conservative majority, but both being marked by the sullen abstention of a third of the electorate, it was, roughly speaking, the liberal, urban haves against the urban and rural have nots and the rural haves. But on other, more directly economic issues — most notably the distrubution of the tax burden which continued to favour farmers and big business

11

against PAYE workers - it was in general a more straight-forward urban - rural divide. With this complex set of conflicts, and with the savage conflict in the North sapping the power of uncomplicated rhetorical nationalism to paper over the cracks, it became, in the eighties, impossible for Irish politics to work the old model which divided the spoils between two conservative nationalist parties each of which depended for its appeal on the notion that it was not a party at all but a national movement, representing all classes and interests at once.

So governments fell like the rain. The eighties began with the main political party Fianna Fail in office with the biggest majority in the history of the state. Yet in the first two years of the decade, the political system that had been among the most stable in Europe became chronically and incurably unstable. By the end of 1982, there had been three general elections. By the end of the decade, there had been five. In none of them did any party succeed in getting an overall parliamentary majority. What had been a 2.5 party system in 1980, Fianna Fail on one side, Fine Gael and its compliant Labour partner on the other, was, by 1989, a five party system, with Labour out on its own and two new parliamentary forces, the Workers Party on the left and the Progressive Democrats on the right. Traditional voting patterns which had held since the end of the Civil War in 1923 collapsed as competing electorates became more ruthless and unsentimental about their own interests.

All of this was a reflection, not a cause, of a wider and deeper cultural instability, of a situation in which it had become impossible to think of Ireland as a unifying concept that would underlie and overhang every social and cultural phenomenon, in which there were many competing and conflicting Irelands on the same island. The sense of Ireland as an invention, a fantasy, as something up for grabs and needing to be refashioned every time a speech was made or a painting begun, became overwhelming. In the early eighties, the acronym for the country was GUBU, Conor Cruise O'Brien's coinage from the description by Charles Haughey of the situation in which the country's most wanted murderer had been found hiding in the flat of the country's most senior law officer, the Attorney General: "grotesque, unbelievable, bizarre and unprecedented". The same Charles Haughey described *his* version of Ireland in a film called "Charles Haughey's Ireland", thus: "When I talk about my Ireland I am talking about something which is not yet a complete reality. It is a dream that has not yet been fulfilled." At the end of his report on the Kerry Babies, the judge who conducted the

12

investigation saw fit to quote James Thurber: "We live, man and worm, in an age where almost everything can mean almost anything..."

In the public language of Ireland in the eighties, the country was a dream, reality was incomplete, events were unbelievable even though they had happened, anything could mean everything, and everything was unprecedented. In cultural terms, the very distinction between a mainstream and an avant garde, between those who wanted to reflect the world and those who wanted to invent new worlds, became meaningless. Since the world itself was so fantastic, so fictional, then to reflect it was to invent it.

This was both the burden and the blessing of Irish culture in the 1980s. A burden because there was so little that could be relied on, that could be taken as read or given or for granted. Tradition could be used only ironically. A thatched cottage on the stage of a new Irish play was not a static backdrop but something that would have to be immediately contradicted and subverted. A statue of the Blessed Virgin in an Irish art photograph was there not for reassurance but for contrast, as a mark of yearning or despair or comic incongruity. A landscape could be painted only to dissolve into a personal, subjective vision. A conventional narrative could be begun only to be joked with: "Spring came early that year — no, I'm wrong, it came late." (John Banville, "Mefisto") If traditional myths had to be used, then they would be not the heroic, collective myths of Cuchulain or Fionn MacCumhail, or of Joyce's Homer but the myths of Sweeney, the maddened existential outsider who was returned to again and again in the eighties in the visual arts, in theatre, in poetry. Myth could be used, not to counteract the sense of fracture and isolation but to re-inforce it.

There is a radical openness about Irish culture after the eighties. Modern Ireland is permeable, economically, culturally, and in terms of population. It lets in the great tide of international blandness and it lets out much of the life blood of the country. But when the identity that is thus undermined is as rigid and narrow and illusory as the Irish one was, then a loss of identity is not necessarily a bad thing. Whereas in the seventies, there was a sense that Irish culture was willing to follow anything that came its way, that it was so insecure that it leaped on any new thing, there was instead a sense in the eighties that Irish culture was willing to *use* anything that came its way, a very different thing. There was a hunger, certainly, but also a greater confidence about being able to absorb and digest things, rather than merely imitate them.

An important part of this openness was the extent to which women began to take their place in the public realm. Politics, business and public affairs were only marginally less male-dominated than they had been before, but within that context women became vastly more active. And if for the culture generally there was little in the way of a usable heritage, for women this need to invent from scratch was compounded by the feeling that what there was in the way of a tradition was not necessarily *theirs*. There was a double need to begin anew, and, because of the international nature of the women's movement, a double incentive to look outwards to a wider context than the immediate Irish one.

The 1980s in Ireland can be seen as a time of retrenchment, a time when, in keeping with the international trend towards a renovated right-wing, the country called a halt to the process of liberalisation and opening which had been underway for two decades. It makes more sense, though, to regard it as a time when the gap between private action and public expression became total. Traditional values needed to be publicly re-inforced precisely because they had ceased to have private meaning. The need for supposedly permanent values, for sets of words enshrined forever in a constitution, is at its greatest when nothing is really permanent. Symbols of stability become crucial in times of instability and in the Ireland of the 1980s instability became almost the most stable fact of life. Emigration, the ultimate expression of an unstable place, became the one thing that remained continuous in Irish life since the nineteenth century. The one thing that was permanent was the sense of impermanence, the sense that one generation would not be able to hand anything on to the next, scattered, generation. In those circumstances only one commandment really held good: start again, make it new, make it better.

A. DESPERADOS

SEEING IS BELIEVING

The revelations that week were disturbing. Sergeant Patrick Reilly told the Kerry Babies Tribunal in Tralee, twenty miles away, of how he had found the body of an infant on the rocks at White Strand. Mrs Mary Hayes said that if her daughter Kathleen had been calling out from the front door to Joanne in the field, the night Joanne had had the baby, she herself had heard nothing. A Professor of Oceanography was asked by James Duggan BL what would happen to an object the size of a newborn infant wrapped in a plastic bag and thrown into the sea off Slea Head. Worst was the evidence of Superintendent John Sullivan, outlining the course of the investigation into the death of the infant found at Cahirciveen, evidence which touched on dark things. They had, he said, checked into cases of incest, of married men known to have been associating with single girls, of a woman who was pregnant and went to England but might have returned. The parents of a girl whose diary contained references to rape were also interviewed. There were even checks on itinerants and hippies. Somebody, he said, had even suggested that it might all be connected with black magic.

When the children of Asdee told their parents of what they had seen in the church, some of them thought of the terrible things that were being dragged to light in Tralee. "There was all that Kerry babies business," says one father "and there have been other things too. There've been two murders in the Listowel area and over in Tarbert there was a case of a man who was having sex with his two neices and got one of them pregnant. That's why some of the people here think that what's happened is a sign. There's a message there and it's to do with all the bad things that have been happening."

At twenty past twelve on the day that Superintendent Sullivan was giving evidence in Tralee, Thursday 14 February, Elizabeth Flynn entered the little church of Saint Mary which is next door to her school in Asdee. Asdee is no more than a dip in the road from Ballybunion to Ballylongford, a tiny line of buildings of which the church, the school, two pubs and the shop-cum-petrol pump are the most notable. From down in the centre of the village's one street there is nothing to be seen but the straggling sparsely populated dairying land around. From the brow of the hill where the village starts, however, the winking towers of industrial Ireland, the power stations of Moneypoint and Tarbet, loom up from the Shannon estuary. And in the estuary the long dark bulk of a 140,000 tonne coal carrier, the biggest ship ever to dock in an Irish port, lies at Moneypoint, clearly visible.

Elizabeth is seven and she goes to the church every day at lunchtime. She is making her first Communion this month. Mrs Eileen Moriarty, the principal teacher in the school is a devout elderly woman and she encourages all her pupils to go next door to the church at lunchtime to "give two or three minutes to Jesus and the church." Elizabeth prayed to the two statues, painted plaster images of the Blessed Virgin and the Sacred Heart which stand in the alcove at the back of the church on the left hand side, separated by a brass trolley, surmounted with votive candles and a small round stained glass porthole which lets in a dim diffuse light. Then she saw the sacred Heart crook his finger and beckon her over to him.

When she looked again, Our Lady's mouth was open.

Martin Fitzgerald, who is ten and is one of the altar boys in the church, was playing "hunting" out at the back of the school when Elizabeth Flynn and other "young ones" came up to him. They told him that the statues were moving. He went in with a large group of other children and looked at the statues for a while. He saw the head and eyes of one of the statues move. Some of the other children who were there at the same time saw nothing. Gradually all of the children gathered into the church to look. Altogether thirty-six of them now say that they saw the statues move in various ways. Some, like Blanaid Quane, have had more than one vision, seeing the statues move on different occasions up to the present. A few of their parents say they too have seen movements in the statues.

In the Jesse James Tavern, next door to Saint Mary's Church, the woman of the house keeps a small hard cover notebook behind the bar. The tavern has a low uneven ceiling, smoke stained walls and a sign on the wall facing the back door that says "Please use the toilet". Apart from the pool table, the juke box and the framed photographs of Jesse James that hang above the fireplace along with a Wanted Dead or Alive Poster, it is an old style village pub. The juke box is on and the air is filled with the nasal tones of Tony Stevens singing a country and western song, Send Me No Roses, the B-side of the local anthem, The Village of Asdee. The notebook

17

behind the bar is the legacy of the man who put Asdee on the map, the former parish priest Father Liam Ferris. It contains, in bold clear handwriting, a romantic version of the life and death of Jesse James, along with stories about his Asdee ancestors collected by Father Ferris from old people around the village.

Father Ferris dominated the village from the Second World War until the end of the sixties, and he always believed that Asdee was marked out for a special distinction. A colourful and unorthodox man, he came to believe that the ancestors of Jesse James had come from Asdee and on 4 April every year he would say a solemn requiem Mass, in the same church where the children would see the moving statues, for the repose of the soul of the greatest desperado of them all. He spent many years researching the connection with the James family. He touched the village with a sense of the extraordinary, and at the same time tried to encourage a simple piety, organising and encouraging devotion to Saint Eoin's holy well, half a mile from the village towards the estuary.

One of the stories in the notebook in the Jesse James Tavern concerns Saint Eoin's Well. In April 1965 Father Ferris wrote a story he had collected under the heading *Blindness*: "The James were Protestants. A servant girl of theirs was going blind and she went to the local holy well. She made a ''round' there and got her sight. At the same time her master had a horse gone blind. He took it to the holy well, and marched it around several times. The horse got its sight, but James, its owner, got blind."

Many people in Asdee still believe in the magical properties of Saint Eoin's well, particularly as a healer of the eyes. They say that some years ago a woman called Ellen Welch was praying there when she saw two fish in the water. She was immediately cured of her illness. They say that when the fish appear again in the water whoever sees them will be cured.

The last Saturday in April is one of the traditional days of worship at the well, a worship revived by Father Ferris. This year a few dozen people had gathered, walking up the winding tarmacadamed boreen and through the small rusting gate set among the hedges where a cardboard sign coloured with a child's hand says "The Holy Well". The well is a shallow pool of clear water fed by a sluggish spring. The thick bushes have been cleared from the water but encroach on three sides. On the fourth side some rough hewn stones serve as a kneeling place for the pilgrims to bend and scoop the blessed water up in a grey smoked glass coffee cup. In front of them at the far side of the pool is a small plaster virgin and child set on a blue and white square of tablecloth on the top of a rickety chair. The surrounding bushes are tied with clean white rags, pagan symbols of the flowering forth of May. The pilgrims mutter incessant rosaries. The following morning they will wait back after Mass at ten and mutter the same rosaries before the statues at the back of Saint Mary's church.

Worship at the well had declined until the arrival of the present curate Father Michael O'Sullivan in Asdee a little over a year ago. He not only revived the worship at the well, but solemnised it, concelebrating Mass there late last summer with two other priests. There was a large turnout from the village and what one villager describes as a "tremendous atmosphere". There was singing in the still air of the holy place and a double rainbow encircled the well while the mass was in progress. Afterwards, a few of the villagers came to see this as a sign, a portent of what was to come.

The Holy Well and the notebook in the Jesse James Tavern are not Father Ferris' only legacies. He invested Asdee with a sense of other worlds. Father Ferris' views of the world were so unorthodox that in ecclesiastical circles the term "feresy" was coined to cover his many sub-heretical opinions.

He believed that all those who attended Mass should share in the sacred mysteries of the priesthood and thus that communion should be given in the hand. He believed that Moses, Plato and Aristotle should be canonised. He wrote a history of the world, *The Story of Man* which featured the French Revolution only as a footnote on page 72. He invented a new world, Pollantory, a place where souls went to have the good knocked out of them before they went to Hell, just as they went to Purgatory to have the bad knocked out of them before they went to Heaven. And once, in one of the sermons in Saint Mary's church, which he would deliver with alternate sentences in English and Irish, he told the people of Asdee, in relation to Jesus walking on the water, that "anyone could walk on the water if they had enough ESB running through their bodies."

Father Ferris' many worlds mingled with the worlds of local folklore which was taught in the school by old Mr Moriarty, who died in 1981, a folklore which still holds a half belief among some of the village people. There are two hundred fairy forts in the vicinity of Asdee and some people claim to have seen lights going from one fort to another. There are stories of a drowned village under the sea between the nearby Beale Strand and Loop Head.

Father Michael O'Sullivan arrived as curate early in 1984. He had been a curate in Texas and had a strong belief in Padre Pio, the

Italian monk who inspired great devotion because he appeared to carry the stigmata of Christ on his body. He himself had come through a serious operation and attributed his deliverence to the intercession of Padre Pio. His arrival sparked off a greater enthusiasm for the church and religion generally. He organised a party of villagers to clean up the small grotto, showing an apparition of the Blessed Virgin, which had fallen into a run-down state. He had Mass said at the Holy Well. And in November he started a Padre Pio prayer group, which would pray fervently every week against the encroaching evils of the world. A few weeks before the miracles of 14 February, Father O'Sullivan had a film about Padre Pio shown in the village and there was a good attendence, including many of the children.

The sacristan is filling the candle stalls at the back of the church with yet another box of votive candles. Forty little flames are flickering around the statues, causing shadowy movements on their painted surfaces. In the three months since the statues moved, the people of the village have come to take the miracles in their stride. "There have been so many miraculous movements in Asdee," says the sacristan "the people don't remark on them much anymore. The only thing we haven't had yet is a cure, and I'm sure that will come. But we've had a lot more movements than Knock has ever had."

There are now almost as many adults as children who claim to have seen movements in the statues - hands lifting, eyes moving, small spots appearing on the Blessed Virgin's neck. Some say they have smelt heavenly perfumes. "It's like a reminder that there is another world," says a woman across the street from the church. "And these things never happen except in poor little places like Asdee and Knock. Our Lady never appeared in Dublin."

Shortly after the movements were seen in Asdee, a group of children in Ballydesmond, a village on Kerry's border with Cork, saw the statues move in *their* local church. The people of Asdee are scornfully amused at the Ballydesmond stories. "Do you know what happened in Ballydesmond a few weeks ago?" asks one local man. "Two young fellas were in praying in the church one evening and the sacristan locked the door without checking if there was anyone inside. Well, a while later, weren't a few others walking down past the church and they heard these figures banging on the windows from the inside. Well they ran like the clappers over to the priest's house shouting, 'Come quick father, the statues are trying to get out of the window'."

On the first Sunday after Asdee's apparitions, there were two thousand people in the village, a bigger crowd even than the one which had gathered the previous September when John Kennedy, who owns the shop and petrol pump in the village, brought home the Sam Maguire cup which he had helped to win as a member of the Kerry football team. Since then the stream of pilgrims has slowed, but it is still steady. And there have been more miracles. A man from Cavan who came on a Thursday evening to celebrate his wedding anniversary reached up to touch the statue of the Blessed Virgin, placing his fingertips on its hand. His finger and thumb, he claimed, were held firm in the statue's grasp for many seconds while he tried to release its hold. A woman who came in a busload from Newry one Sunday felt the Blessed Virgin take her hand in her own. The statue's hand, she said, turned to warm flesh as it gripped her. She was crying uncontrollably.

The miracles are noted down and placed through Father O'Sullivan's letterbox. Father O'Sullivan refers all queries to the diocesan office. Matters have been taken out of his hands. For the first few Sundays there were Stations of the Cross in the church and the rosary was relayed outside to the waiting crowds on a loudspeaker. The speaker still juts from the pebble-dashed church wall but it is now silent. Local people say that the order came from the bishop that the rosary was no longer to be relayed outside.

Many villagers still expect a message. Some thought there would be a message at Easter. When it didn't come, they simply carried on. "There will surely be a message," says a man whose daughter had two visions. "With all that's happening it wouldn't make sense if there was no message."

The pilgrims and petitioners who come are drawn not by miracles, but by the mundane miseries of the everyday world. From half past two on Sunday they bow their heads and step humbly into the twilight zone around the statues, the light from outside refracted from the rain and strained through the coloured glass. The older women cover their heads and mumble rosaries in unison. The younger women and most of the men stand stock still staring at the plaster images, their eyes not revealing whether they are daring or begging the statues to move. Red plump children play on the floor, their frustration held in check by occasional warnings.

Sometimes the petitioners scribble notes and leave them at the foot of either statue, mostly that of the Blessed Virgin. A woman leaves a leaflet that proclaims the power of Holy Water - "the devil cannot long abide in a place or near a person that is often sprinkled with this blessed water." But mostly the petitions are more personal.

21

"Our Blessed Lady, please bless all my family and help us sort out all our problems. Make Mam, Dad, better again and let us be one big family together forever." "Please, please, help Jim to stop drinking and give us peace in our home." "Sacred Heart of Jesus, grant all my intentions and help me pay my bills." They fondle the hands of the statues continually, rubbing and stroking them. A woman takes a small white child's vest from her bag and rubs it to the statue of the Sacred Heart, then quickly replaces it and moves through the door. Now and then another candle gutters out and sends a last exhalation of smoke towards the roofbeams.

Magill, May, 1985.

OUR LADY
QUEEN OF KNOCK

"Oh my Jesus, forgive us our sins, save us from the fires of hell and lead all souls to Heaven, especially those in need of thy mercy." The first rosary is ending as the bus draws into Kinnegad. Margaret Lewis, in white veil and wimple embroidered with a golden rose, white stockings and white shoes, leads the prayers. The rose is a symbol of purity, her uniform that of a Handmaid of Knock Shrine. All summer long she travels up and down, tending the crippled and the sick on their way to Knock. Though the summer is long over, she has organised this pilgrimage for the last great feast day of the year - the Immaculate Conception.

There are no invalids on the bus, though Mrs Eileen Carleton who sits with her husband is still recuperating. Deaf in one ear since the age of seven, she has recently undergone a miraculous cure. She mixed holy water from Knock with some clay from the gable wall where the apparition was seen and put it on the deaf ear. A few nights later she put her hand over her good ear and realised that she could still hear the television. "She nearly went wild with the shock," says her husband. "I thought she was having another turn. We used to pray mostly to Padre Pio before, but we're devoted to Our Lady of Knock now."

As each decade begins, it is offered for a special intention - a house, a job, a safe recovery from illness, a happy family. "I've just had a letter," announces Mrs Lewis "from the General of the Blue Army in Australia. He especially asks us to pray for peace. There are also two priests who asked me to remember them in our prayers. One is dying of cancer and the other died a week ago." Mrs Kenny sits in beside me to relate another miracle. "It's about a man called Jack Murray. He was away from Holy Communion for many years when he was off living in England. His wife was always praying that he would come back to the faith. When he was home on holidays they took him down to Knock. The day after he was going out in the morning. 'Where are you going?' his brother asked him. 'I'm going to confession.' He had a stroke shortly afterward and he died in a hospice in Harold's Cross. He died a beautiful death."

Margaret Lewis was sleeping fitfully. Her mind was troubled. At the age of two, her first-born child, a son, was seriously ill, his hip eaten away by disease. In her dream she saw a woman in white with a crown on her head, her hands opening out towards heaven. She went towards the woman and said "Mary of divine purity, cure my son." The woman told her to sneeze three times. Margaret Lewis awoke sneezing. On Christmas Eve she poured some clay from the gable of the Church of the Apparition at Knock, given to her by a friend of her brother's, into a suppurating wound on her son's hip. By St Stephen's Day, the wound was healed. She knew then that it was to Knock she must look for the cure of her son's tuberculosis.

For fifteen years, she brought her son to Knock, herself tending to the sick as a Handmaid. When he was seventeen the long-awaited miracle occured. On Rosary Sunday in the Marian Year they visited the shrine. Next morning, his leg, which had no hip joint because of the disease, had grown three inches. A new hip joint was grafted on and a blood test revealed that he was completely free of tuberculosis. When the Pope visited Knock, she told his private secretary about the cure. "This is the kind of thing the Pope wants to hear," Father Magee told her. Afterwards she wrote to Rome and had a warm letter in return from the Pope himself.

Since that day in 1954, miracles have woven themselves into the fabric of Margaret Lewis's life. Every good fortune which comes her family's way, she attributes to the power of Our Lady of Knock. Her life is devoted to the shrine. "I do nothing else. I don't go to pictures, dances, drink or smoke. It's my whole life." Our Lady has countered every misfortune. "My husband got a sore on the side of his nose, outside, and when it was spreading, and not showing any signs of healing, we consulted a doctor who had the nose examined and the test proved the growth was malignant. By the end of nine months, regardless of all the treatment, the sore was worse. There was a constant discharge from it and a very offensive odour. It was then we thought of asking the help of Our Lady of Knock. He went on pilgrimage to Knock Shrine and fasted all day as an act of penance. Next morning we found to our great joy that the cancer had healed overnight, and he has never had the slightest recurrence."

In New Jersey last year, showing films of the Pope's visit to Knock, she fell down two flights of stairs, fracturing two ribs and hurting her back. When she returned to Ireland she became paralysed from the waist down. "I was a week in Mercer's Hospital when they took X-rays and discovered the back injuries. That

24

morning, at six o' clock the doctor gave me two tablets. That morning I prayed to Our Lady and to Archdeacon Kavanagh, who was parish priest of Knock at the time of the apparition, and the next morning I was walking. The doctor said 'I don't know whether to put it down to Knock Shrine or medical science.'"

"I was born thirty five miles from here. When I was a young lad my parents were Catholics of course and they were very religious. They were people who said the Rosary every night. My grandfather always led the Rosary, and it was said in Irish. And my mother said the litany and other trimmings. I was a good Catholic lad. I was a Mass server, took a great interest in Mass, took a great interest in my prayers. As a boy if ever I was in trouble I would go to my mother before I would go to my father. I would talk to her. Mary is our mother. She is our spiritual mother.

"I went to school in Partry, and Partry is a beautiful place between two lakes, between Lough Mask and Lough Carra. In my young days I often amused myself by going out boating with the people. There were boats on both lakes and I often went fishing. I wasn't a fisherman really. I hadn't the patience. I suppose like Saint Peter and the Apostles I became a fisher of men. I wasn't very good at the other kind of fishing.

"We often came to Knock, and we came by sidecar, and I remember as a child that I would fall asleep in the car and I wouldn't wake up again until we had arrived at our house at home. When I got older and when I was able to cycle, I came to Knock with another boy, Tommy Walsh, who lived in the next village to me. We started off on the evening of the fourteenth of August and we came along to Knock for the fifteenth. The fifteenth is the feast of the Assumption. It is one of the big days in Knock. It was the pilgrimage day for everybody at that time. I remember parking my bicycle up the road here. I know the house where I parked my bicycle. The same house is not there now but there is a house in its place. It cost me sixpence to park my bicycle and then we went around. There was a big crowd milling around the church. They were doing the traditional station. First they visit the Blessed Sacrament. Then they walk around the church and say fifteen mysteries of the Rosary, and then do the Stations of the Cross and then visit the Blessed Sacrament again. We did all that. During that night we went to Confession, we received Communion. The first Mass in the morning was at six o' clock and we went to that, and then we cycled home and that was a distance of thirty five miles. I was a young lad that time and I was a student at Saint Jarlath's

College. I was about fifteen years of age. I never thought for one moment that I would ever be here as parish priest."

The voice of Monsignor James Horan P.P., parish priest of Knock, booms out from the loudspeakers that jut out from the humble tower of the Church of the Apparition: "I would like to welcome also the pilgrimage from Dublin led by Mrs Lewis who has done great work for the shrine over so many years." Anti-clockwise round the church the pilgrims walk, some praying aloud, others silently. At the fourth stage of the Traditional Station they halt before the Apparition Gable where Patrick Hill and the other visionaries saw the Virgin: "She wore a brilliant crown on her head, and over the forehead, where the crown fitted the brow, a beautiful robe. The crown appeared brilliant and of a golden brightness, of a deeper hue, inclined to a mellow yellow, than the striking whiteness of the robe she wore..."

At the Apparition Gable the pilgrims halt to murmur the Litany of the Blessed Virgin: Holy Mother of God, Holy Virgin of Virgins, Mother of Christ, Mother of Divine Grace, Mother most pure, Mother most chaste, Mother inviolate, Mother undefiled, Mother most amiable, Mother of our Creator, Mother of Good Counsel, Mother of our Saviour, Virgin most prudent, Virgin most venerable, Virgin most renowned, Virgin most powerful, Virgin most merciful, Virgin most faithful, Mirror of Justice, Seat of Wisdom, Cause of our Joy, Spiritual vessel, Vessel of honour, Singular vessel of devotion, Mystical rose, Tower of David, Tower of Ivory, House of Gold, Ark of the Covenant, Gate of heaven, Morning star, Health of the sick, Refuge of sinners, Comforter of the afflicted, Help of Christians, Queen of Angels, Queen of Patriarchs, Queen of Prophets, Queen of Apostles, Queen of Martyrs, Queen of Confessors, Queen of Virgins, Queen of all Saints, Queen conceived without original sin, Queen assumed into heaven, Queen of the most holy Rosary, Queen of Peace. "Please cease your private devotions," orders the voice from the loudspeaker. "You may resume them later. Make way for the public ceremonies." They crowd into a little church, packing all three aisles, leaving hardly room to breathe. The Monsignor disappears into the sacristy, leaving three curates to celebrate the Mass. "We recognise our own sinfulness, our own failure," says the preacher.

The area around the shrine looks like an airport, although the real one is being built eight miles away. The vast assembly area stretches out like a runway and the Basilica of Our Lady Queen of Ireland is a huge, looming hangar. Everywhere are signposts and information huts. This way to the confessional chapel (thirty seven confessionals employing twenty five priests full time in the summer season), that way for advice on the Billings Method. Another new church is half built. Everywhere it is efficient and unsentimental. A sign in the toilets says "Please help with the maintenance and upkeep of the toilets by putting a coin in the box." The hawkers' barrows have made way for bright open religious goods shops, each fronted with an identical brown fringe marked with the name of a different saint. In the Knock Shopping Arcade (restaurant and knick-knack pedlars; fish fingers and chips *2.95) a coloured picture of the Pope is marked on the back "Try our wines, ports, sherries".

"Knock is an oasis of peace and religious joy," says Monsignor Horan. "It is an oasis of prayer, an oasis of intercession through Our Lady to Almighty God. She is here. She came to Knock on 21 August 1879 when Ireland was in much the same type of situation that she is now. There was a lot of violence, there was a lot of murder, there was a lot of intimidation. The Irish people that time, let's face it, were only second class citizens. They couldn't own their own land, they couldn't improve their own land or if they did the landlord would put extra taxes on them. There was violence because there wasn't justice. You need peace with justice. Our Lady came then. She appeared here at Knock. She had her family with her. She was dressed in white with a cloak tied here at the neck. She had a crown on her head with a rose at the verge of the crown and the forehead, which is a symbol of purity, of chastity. Our Lady was praying for the Irish people, that they might settle their differences in some orderly way, in some democratic way. Perhaps it was a dawning of the day, that they should settle their differences not in a violent way but through prayer and through religion.

"Things were never as bad since that day because Davitt came that spring, or even that particular August there was a meeting in Irishtown, a Land League meeting. And then afterwards Charles Stewart Parnell joined the movement, and in 1886 there was relief for the farmers - the Land Act was passed. The rest is history. You had the Irish Volunteers and you had the Second World War. I hope that Our Lady at Knock is still praying for the Irish people, that there'll be a solution to the North, that we'll get peace which will bring prosperity. We are a people with a great heritage, a great Christian heritage."

The Monsignor will not say whether miracles occur at Knock. "There are," he says "two different ways in which God can cure people. He can cure people through the ordinary natural healing powers in our bodies. Or he can cure them in a supernatural way, when somebody is healed quickly, gets up and walks. Like the miracles Our Lord performed in Palestine. We're thinking of setting up a medical bureau but then Our Lord didn't bring around a medical bureau with him when he went around Palestine."

Whether they are cured or not, the sick are happy. "One thing I learned about the sick is - what is happiness? Happiness doesn't mean good health, it doesn't mean wealth, it doesn't mean that you have everything in the world that you want. Because I find that the sick are the happiest people I know. Because they have perfect resignation to God's will. As long as we are opposing God's will, there's a struggle, there's a conscious struggle. But once you accept God's will and go along with God's will, there is no struggle. You are fully happy. I met a woman over there and she was thirty years on a stretcher. Not only was she on a stretcher, but her head could only turn in one direction and her hands were crippled so she had to be spoon-fed. And she was one of the happiest people I know. She was perfectly happy. Suffering can bring great happiness and great fulfillment."

On the eve of the Feast of the Immaculate Conception, Deirdre Manifold was at Knock Shrine to take part in the prayer vigil organised by the Apostolate of Atonement for Abortion. She brought with her copies of her book "Fatima and the Great Conspiracy" to sell. Many years ago, in the middle of a crisis of faith, Deirdre Manifold came to Knock and witnessed a miracle. Before the Apparition Gable a young girl in a communion dress who had not walked for years rose from her wheelchair and began to walk. "I was looking straight at her. I could have been looking over there or over there but I was looking directly at her. God was teaching me a lesson." She was confirmed in her faith, but she felt sure that events in the world were unfolding according to the designs of an evil power beyond her grasp. "The war made a very deep impact on my mind. I felt that the ordinary people everywhere didn't want war. I had an intuitive idea that if 99.9 percent of people didn't want to go to war, then .001 percent of people were able to make them go to war, unknown to themselves. Whoever controlled the world's money controlled the world."

Working in the civil service in Dublin in the late forties and early fifties, she joined the Legion of Mary and a right-wing political movement called National Action which stood a candidate in the election of 1954. From there she made contact with other people

28

around the country who shared her belief that there was a great conspiracy to take over the world in operation all the time. She began to subscribe to American publications of the far-right. A few years ago she imported three hundred copies of a book called "None Dare Call It Conspiracy" expounding the theory that we are all victims of a conspiracy to foist communism on the world. The conspirators are the Insiders, controlled from Moscow and including in their ranks Richard Nixon and the Rockefellers.

"I would pick up hitchhikers, mostly students, in my car, and talk to them about world events. Then I'd reach into the glove compartment and give them a copy of 'None Dare Call It Conspiracy'."Here read that. If you go back to your own area and if you tell people what I've been telling you, the Insiders can't stop us doing that. They have control of everything else. But they can't stop us talking, at least not yet. The day may come when they'll have the car bugged." She continued her work as a Handmaid of Knock Shrine.

On New Year's Day this year Deirdre Manifold was talking to a friend. Both were in some trouble - her husband was dying and so was his wife. "Do you accept the accidental theory of history or do you believe in the Insider-Conspiratorial theory of history?" she asked suddenly. She explained her view of the Great Conspiracy. "When you go back to your school in Kilkenny, tell the other teachers and the students any way you can," she urged. "By the end of the century how many would you have told?" he asked wryly. She decided to write a book and had two thousand copies printed. At the vigil in Knock she sold all she had brought with her. In five weeks, the entire first edition was sold out. She is printing a second edition and also publishing a re-issue of the anti-abortion book "Babies For Burning" which had to be withdrawn from sale in Britain some years ago because of libellous inaccuracies.

"Fatima and the Great Conspiracy" is based on "None Dare Call It Conspiracy" and on the monthly newsletter of the Christian Anti-Communism Crusade ("The Communist plan for the conquest of the USA is: External encirclement, plus internal demoralisation, plus thermonuclear blackmail, leads to progressive surrender." "The only way to be sure you don't get herpes is: refrain from sexual relations. Stay a virgin, marry a virgin and remain faithful to each other."). "When I was in Fatima I met Joe Lovell from Longford and Joe has brought out a book called 'Miracles'. I said to Joe 'How did you distribute your book?'. 'Well' he said 'I looked up at Our Lady and I said to her I don't know how to distribute this book but

29

you do.' He told me to do the same and it has certainly worked. Our Lady is a good saleswoman."

"There must be a spiritual answer to every secular question. It would be unfair of Christ to found a church that could err. It would be unfair of Christ to leave us in a position where we couldn't solve the problem of unemployment or the national debt. But he hasn't. The Church has the answers. It has the answer to the moral problems but it has the answer to the financial and social questions as well. Knock renews people's faith in the Church. The vision of Knock is very important for this century. It's only when the laws of this country are in conformity with the laws of the Church that there'll be peace.

"The devil was never as active as he is now. At the very dawn of creation didn't God say to the devil 'I will put enmity between you and the woman, between thy seed and her seed. She shall crush thy head and you shall lie in wait for her heel.' I would see this insider conspiracy as a powerhouse. We'll take it as two opposite poles - if we could bring it into geographical or physical terms, I would see the Mother of God as she is made manifest at Fatima and Knock at one side of the globe throwing out wires and cables every side, criss-crossing, bringing grace. And I would see evil as a powerhouse on the opposite side fighting against it at every turn."

On the morning of the Feast of the Immaculate Conception, while the pilgrims' bus was pulling in for tea and biscuits at Kinnegad, Monsignor Horan was preaching a sermon to the villagers of Knock, the ones he calls "my people". "We're living in a very permissive world," he was saying. "We're living in a world where there is lots of controversy about different things. We're living also in a world where the youth are confused. They're having all sorts of propaganda thrown at them from the box in the kitchen. On this Feast of the Immaculate Conception I want to tell you a story about way back in 1629. People believed in the Immaculate Conception that time although it wasn't defined until 1824 and Pius IX. But Ferdinand the Third of Austria was worried about his empire because the Swedish Army had broken into Europe and they were drunk with victories and they were knocking at the gates of the Empire. So he thought that he would do something about it, spiritually. And he raised a huge monument in honour of Our Lady in the Square of Vienna and he had a statue of Our Lady on top of the monument and her foot on the satanic serpent. And he brought all the dignitaries of state and all the dignitaries of church together and he had a dedication ceremony and they dedicated it to God and to Our Lady. And lo and behold when they confronted the enemy at the Battle of Eger, Ferdinand won and he made peace with the enemy. His prayer was answered.

"And at this time in our country we have invaders as well. You have in your own kitchen, your own sitting room. You have a box there and you have people putting forward all kinds of theories. Whether it is about the permissive society, or about abortion, or contraception, or divorce, or drugs or immoral cinema, pornographic literature - all these things. And these enemies are more subtle. Ferdinand the Third could see his enemies. He knew where they were. But the enemies in our society as far as Christian morality and our Irish heritage is concerned, you don't know who your enemies are. They work secretly, they work silently, they work through pressure groups. Maybe Our Lady as she helped Ferdinand the Third might help us to solve our problems. I think the thing we most need is some kind of political movement in the country." Knock Shrine is Monsignor Horan's Vienna monument, his powerhouse against evil.

Monsignor Horan likes politicians. He has met Charles Haughey twice and thinks very highly of him. He would have done great things if only he'd been given the chance. "I never mention politics outside this house," he adds. "I'm very disappointed when I hear people talking on television about a priest-ridden society. I think if you look at it from a certain point of view, it's a people-ridden society. Because the priest has been a marvellous stand-by for the people of his parish. I'm not a politician, I lobby politicians. I lobby to get things for the people in this parish. I lobby them to get things that would improve the condition of the people in the west of Ireland. I'm involved in an airport now that would be marvellous infrastructure for the west. I like dealing with politicians. Whoever is Taoiseach I give him full loyalty and full co-operation. It's a combination of the priests with the politicians. I think it's traditional for priests to take an interest in their people. If I am interested in the people's welfare, in their families, in their happiness, then they'll trust me. They'll know that I am their friend. And if I preach to them, they'll know that I'm sincere in what I'm saying. It's a tradition in Ireland that the priest is a leader amongst his people, and that they look up to the priest."

If Knock is an oasis of prayer, then the only bar open in the village is an oasis of a different kind. There's drink, a pool table and a girlie calendar on the wall. "I think when the airport is finished," muses the barman "I'll move my plane over from Castlebar to here.

It'll be very handy for me." On the television in the corner, Tony McMahon is playing "Anach Cuain", the west's great hymn of sorrow. "You know," says the barman "the Monsignor fancies himself on the accordion too. One night he took it out at a concert beyond. He played 'The Coolin'. Now do you know anything about Irish music? Well, 'The Coolin' is a real difficult tune to play, even if you're good. Oh now this was good all right. There was an oul' fella there that's a real traditional musician himself. You could see he was in agony. He just spat on the floor, pulled down the cap over his face and took a suck out of his pipe. But when the Monsignor was finished, the oul' fella sure clapped like everybody else."

In Dublin. December, 1982.

THE WORLD, THE FLESH
AND EAMON de VALERA

"Try to imagine how I felt. The Christian Brothers had taught me the old Catechism and I learned it, not because I was forced to but because I wanted to. In those days you learned Catholicism, mark you not this stuff they call 'Religion' or 'Christian Doctrine'. Then all of a sudden, when I go to Mass, there's some new change every week. I had learned that the Faith was everlasting, that the Mass could not be changed. Our Lord said 'Upon this rock I shall build my church and the gates of hell shall not prevail against it'. Now they are chipping away at the rock, removing whole chunks of it and the demons from Hell are upon the earth."

Father Michael Cox, ordained into the order of the Mother of God in 1978 by rebel Bishop Revas in Switzerland, is explaining why he rejects the reforms of the Second Vatican Council and upholds the Tridentine Rite.

"The Tridentine Mass," he says "is strong against the Devil. As a priest, I exercise all the powers that God has given me, including exorcism. I have performed two exorcisms. People get the wrong idea about that from all these silly films. It is a casting out of the Devil and it is for the good of the person involved. One of the exorcisms was of the pirate radio station 'Big D' - they were playing terrible filth over the air. One was a song called 'Spanish Train' by Chris de Burgh about God and the Devil playing cards for the souls of the dead; another was something about Eva Peron and it started off with 'Salve Regina', making a mockery of the 'Hail Holy Queen'; the other one was Mick Jagger singing 'The Girl with the Faraway Eyes' which brought in the 'bleeding wounds of Jesus' and how he sent money to a church and got his girl. I like some pop songs myself but I can't understand what makes them do these things. I had to cast the devil out of that place and out of those people." Did he not have to go to the studio to perform the exorcism? "No," he said "there are no barriers to the power of God."

Pope John Paul II told Irish youth in Galway that Satan would be using "all of his might and all of his deceptions to win Ireland for the ways of the world" and Father Cox says that people in Ireland

33

still value the power of the priesthood against "the World, the Flesh and the Devil". He was retired out of the Army after an accident and now has a small pension. "When I was in Saint Brican's Military Hospital," he recalls "some of the nurses gave me a hard time. They kept calling me 'Mr Cox' or just 'Cox' and I told them that I would not tolerate being called anything else but 'Father Cox'. A group of patients went to the hospital chaplain and said: 'Give us a yes-or-no-answer. Is he or is he not a priest?' And he said 'Well yes, he is a valid priest even though he is in rebellion'. After that all the others treated me with more respect. I heard confessions and said Mass. All the Army Officers that used to call me 'Coxy' had a great amount of time for me now, and called me 'Father Cox'. I was driven out to Colaiste Caomhin, the Army administration centre, to get official confirmation that I was a priest. When I came back I held it up and said 'There you are lads - it's official.' There were about thirty-five people in the ward and they all cheered."

Father Cox belongs to a different order to that of the Society of Saint Pius X, founded and led by the chief spokesman for the traditionalists, Archbishop Marcel Lefebvre but espouses the same teachings. The Society of Saint Pius X has a regular congregation of one hundred and fifty in Ireland and on one Sunday every month they gather in the Central Hotel for the celebration of Mass according to the Tridentine Rite by one of the Society's English priests, normally Father Black or Father Gierak. On the other three Sundays, they attend Mass in their local parishes, but only under protest, mindful of the decree of the Council of Trent regarding the Tridentine Rite upon which Lefebvre bases his opposition to the New Liturgy: "We specifically warn all persons, of whatever dignity or rank, Cardinals not excluded, and command them, as a matter of strict obedience never to use or permit any ceremonies or Mass prayers other than the ones contained in this Missal... and determine that this our present order and decree is to last in perpetuity and can never be legally amended or revoked at a future date."

Those who gather once a month are humble and sober. The men in plain Sunday suits, the women with heads covered and bowed, the children prim and obedient, move their lips to the words in the old, well-thumbed black missals or whisper secret, silent prayers of their own. The priest addresses Heaven, not the congregation, which is present merely as a witness. In the cold, bare room, there is an atmosphere of grudging conspiracy, of a persecuted sect sharpening its resistance against the World, the Flesh and the Devil. After the Mass, they sing: "Faith of our fathers, holy faith/ We will be true to thee till death/...In spite of dungeon, fire and sword."

There are two contrasting sounds associated with the Latin Mass: the crystalline, celestial voice of the beautiful Latin plainsong soars above the downcast murmurs and humble aspirations of the congregation. At the Central Hotel, four professional singers in the ante-room add drama and solemnity to the high points of the Mass with the sacred compositions of Palestrina. Across the Liffey, at the weekly sung Latin Mass in the Pro-Cathedral, the song of ages rings out above the reticent responses of the large congregation, below the massive altar-piece of the Ascension depicting a bright, omnipotent God rising in his cloud away from the wretched-looking apostles.

But there are other sounds in the Pro-Cathedral. The dropping of coins on the collection plates echoes almost exactly the clinking of the censer as it produces small clouds of incense that waft about the altar. "The Offertory collection," says the priest "will be a special collection in aid of the Sick and Indigent Roomkeepers' Association." A middle-aged man in a business suit, wearing gold-rimmed glasses, transfers the coins from each plate into a large basket which he discreetly covers with an embroidered white cloth as he makes his way to the sacristy.

The priest is young and bearded, with a strong, melodious singing voice, the sort you would expect to see presiding at a Folk Mass, but he seems confident and comfortable with the Latin rite. There are modern intrusions, however: the rite is a Latin translation of the New Liturgy, the priest faces the people, and two nuns help with the distribution of Communion. On the polished brass trolleys at the back of the church, the threepenny votive candles have been replaced by little red electric lamps that light up when you put in the money.

For all that, the motives of those who attend the Pro-Cathedral Latin Mass regularly are the same as those of Lefebvre's followers. Sean White, a man in his late fifties, told me: "I'm not happy going to these new-fangled Masses at all. The Latin Mass is part of what I believe in. It is part of our history. It was the Mass of the Penal days, said by persecuted priests on Mass Rocks around the country. Those priests kept us alive as a nation and gave us the guts to fight. They're turning out priests now that wouldn't make good altar boys. I was brought up on Jones' Road, beside the Clonliffe Seminary. I'll never forget the sight of the seminarians when they went out

35

walking together early in the morning. Fine straight men they were, with long, black coats lined with red silk. You could tell from the way they were walking that they knew they had the goods. The hands that consecrated the host would never maul a woman."

It was the power of the priest that Archbishop Lefebvre dwelt upon during his pastoral visit to his Irish followers this year. The liberalism of Vatican II, he told them, has led to a "destruction of all authority." "The New Mass is a democratic Mass; the old Mass is a hierarchical Mass. In the New Mass, the priest is reduced to being merely the president of the assembly. He turns towards the faithful instead of towards God." Because of this, he maintains, "God's law is less observed in the State" and the "authority of the State, of the Church, of the father of the family" is threatened. Lefebvre's followers were pleased, however, by Pope John Paul II's "Letter to Priests" in which he examined the difference between "the common priesthood of the faithful" and the "hierarchical priesthood" and chose to reinforce the latter.

Lefebvre's followers and other traditionalists see the world as a place of evil and chaos where the values and forms which they hold to be ordained by God are in danger of being swamped by the forces of the Devil. For that reason, any diminution or dilution of the power and authority, the order and hierarchy, of the Church, is horrible and inexplicable. The World, The Flesh and the Devil can only be fought with the pure unadultered traditions that have preserved God's people thoughout the ages. Life for them is one continuing exorcism. Theirs is a strong sense of persecution and as they see the world, persecution is the result of the separation of Church and State. Their biggest fear, and their source of inspiration, is the vision of a Catholic people subjected by foreign oppression, Communist government, or both. In this at least, the present Pope, as a Polish Catholic, is at one with them.

On the day that Monsignor Horan of Knock, the man who brought Pope John Paul to Ireland, was unveiling a plaque at the birthplace of the ubiquitous Charles Haughey, Mrs Dunne, a well-spoken, middle-aged lady, more usually to be seen preaching to passers-by on "Our Lady's Island" in O'Connell Street, was leaning out of the window of a car driving through the town, waving a large tricolour, and shouting "Freedom for Lithuanian Catholics". A few weeks ago, she was among a group of about a dozen people demonstrating outside the Soviet Ambassador's home in Ailesbury Road in support of Lithuanian Catholics. (The Marian statue in O'Connell Street was originally intended as a gift to Lithuania but the Soviet government refused it.) "We must support the poor Lithuanians," she said.'"We in Ireland know all about what it is like to be denied our religion and our independence. We are no longer persecuted ourselves but the Church in Lithuania is." The organiser of the protest, Mr T.C.G. O'Mahony, a fervently Catholic and anti-Communist solicitor with extreme right-wing connections, refused to be interviewed.

The idea of a nationalism that is intimately connected to religious martyrdom is well rooted in Ireland. Just before his own martyrdom, Patrick Pearse explicitly linked his sufferings to those of Christ: "Dear Mary that did see thy first-born son/Go forth to die amidst the scorn of men/Receive my first-born son into thy arms/Who hath also gone out to die for men/And keep him by thee till I come to him." Archbishop Lefebvre knew he would strike a chord with his Irish audience when he told them that the troubles in the North arose from the betrayal of Catholic principles to Protestantism: "Once you admit the Protestant doctrines, then you bring in destructive forces." Eamon de Valera, survivor of a martyred generation, repaid his debts to the Church by writing a specifically Catholic constitution in consultation with John Charles McQuaid. One of de Valera's biographers, Mary C. Bromage, noted of him that "his strictures extended beyond the evils of drink, to the evil of Jazz, the evils of betting on races, the dangers of indecent books, and he concurred in the Government's Bill to censor publications."

Lefebvre and the other traditionalists see the Irish Constitution as an important bulwark against the rising tide of immorality: divorce, contraception, abortion. Speaking in Dublin, Lefebvre recalls the framers of the 1937 Constitution fondly. He remembers the occasion of the centenary of Rockwell College, when he concelebrated Mass as Superior-General of the Holy Ghost Fathers with Archbishop McQuaid, de Valera acting as server. He pays tribute to the latter as an "exceptional Catholic, a man of great faith and simplicity" and of McQuaid, his "great friend", he says that but for Vatican II, he would certainly have been made Cardinal. It was McQuaid, returning from Vatican II, who told his flock: "Allow me to reassure you. No change will worry the tranquility of your Christian lives."

John Power, chairman of Lefebvre's followers in Ireland, shares his view of the rise of immorality in the world. He is a well dressed businesssman, with a slight air of desperation in spite of his red, two-point-eight-litre Jaguar. "The ten commandments," he says sadly "are being replaced with the ethics of the farmyard. A gross and obscene Family Planning Act is being foisted on a Catholic people by

37

a weak government and already we are hearing the din of those clamouring for divorce in our ears. Thank goodness devotion to Mary has not died out yet. The maintenance of the Rosary is our best hope." Another traditionalist explained the errors of contraception and abortion: "Don't these people know that from the moment a man has - excuse me for saying it, but it has to be said - sexual intercourse with a woman, and a child is conceived, a new soul appears in Heaven, an immortal soul? And the child is already upon the earth. People who use contraceptives are trying to take away God's right to give life, when they should be thanking God for the life he has given them."

John Power is very hopeful that Archbishop Lefebvre will be accepted back into the Church and the Tridentine Rite legalised. Whereas Pope Paul VI had strongly denounced Lefebvre, John Paul II merely remarked that "it is perhaps a good thing that the spokesmen for these opinions should express their fears. However, in this respect also, correct limits must be maintained." Moreover, John Paul has appointed Cardinal Semper as a special go-between with Lefebvre. "We are very hopeful for Pope John Paul," says Power. "His Grace strongly approves of the halt on the laicisation of priests and of his restoration of discipline in the convents. Archbishop Lefebvre is not a rebel like Schillebeeck and Kung. Those priests are in open confrontation with the Church." The traditionalists were also particularly pleased with the Pope's Limerick speech, and its emphatic opposition to divorce and contraception.

Speaking to a Dublin audience, Lefebvre said: "If the Church fails to affirm the principle of making the State follow the law of God, its defences are weakened. The State suffers too - the strength of a country is in its moral fibre. Social order must be preserved. Divorce, contraception and abortion lead to a breakdown in order." When he had finished, an old man politely stopped him, produced a copy of the 1937 Constitution and asked Lefebvre to sign it. When I asked him why, he said: "I am a small farmer from the West and I fought like a good many more for Ireland's freedom. I fought for de Valera in the Civil War. This Constitution was what we fought for and I wanted his Lordship to sign it because he's for the real old faith. You're too young to know it. I have six fine children and they've all done well but they're only lukewarm about their religion. They don't understand what it's like when you don't have the freedom to do as your conscience tells you."

In Dublin. December, 1980.

38

ON THE SIDE OF THE ANGELS
The thoughts of Desmond Connell, Dublin's new Archbishop

The week after his appointment as the new Archbishop of Dublin, Dr Des Connell's colleagues in the Department of Metaphysics at UCD held a small going-away party for him. As usual, the guest of honour spoke briefly of his attachment to the department, of his genuine regret at leaving it, of the pleasure which his work there had given him. His colleagues knew that he was completely sincere, that not only was he sad at leaving but that he was fearful of what might become of his beloved department in his absence. His parting words were "I leave you with the hope that this department will never become a department of contemporary European Philosophy."

No one thought that he might be joking, for anyone who knows his thought knows that not only contemporary philosophy, but a good deal of contemporary theology, including Catholic theology, is anathema to him, dangerous and bordering on the heretical. On all of the moral and dogmatic questions which will face the million Catholics of his diocese over the next decade, Desmond Connell's thought has been formed, not by the modern world but by the work of a thirteenth century saint, Thomas Aquinas. And that thought he sees not just as an option, or a theory, but as a higher order of truth, the mastery of which gives him a special right to be listened to.

Des Connell's first utterances in public print show an impatience with the modern world in which mass communication gives all sorts of people the right to be heard on subjects which he believes they know nothing about. Writing in the Jesuit journal Studies in the autumn of 1957 on the subject of "Saint Thomas and the Future of Metaphysics" he complains of the phenomenon of unqualified people talking about religious matters on the radio. "To take but one example, there is a need (so obvious on this side of the Atlantic to those who have listened to BBC discussions) for a science whose competence to speak on such questions as the existence of God and the immortality of the human soul would command the same universal respect as the competence of the experimental sciences within their own fields. If this need could be satisfied, then might the 'millions' be guided in their attitude to such questions by those only whose metaphysical formation entitles them to be heard."

What it is crucial to understand in relation to Des Connell is that he believes that such an absolute science exists and that he is a practitioner of it. "A metaphysics based upon the principles of Saint Thomas ... is truly scientific ... It preaches the authentic subject matter of a distinct and universal science, properly equipped to demonstrate its conclusions concerning ultimate problems."Thomism (the set of ideas based on the writings of Thomas Aquinas) is "a scientific challenge to agnosticism". His own thoughts, therefore, and the principles to which he adheres, are not speculations about the mysteries of life but scientific discoveries which have the same absolute and incontrovertible status as Boyle's Law or the Law of Gravity. And those who have not been trained in this science have no right to be heard by the "millions".It is not the frame of mind of a man likely to interpret the Church after Vatican 2 as some within it would like to see it: a community of equals, "the people of God"in which there is room for doctrinal debate and individual conscience.

Saint Thomas Aquinas and the scholastic thinkers who followed him in mediaeval times were very much concerned with defining the exact nature of angels, and this debate on angels is at the core of Desmond Connell's major published work, (The Vision in God), published in Louvain and in Paris in 1967. The book is a study of a French philosopher of the seventeenth century, Nicolas Malebranche, and it is concerned to show that Malebranche was heavily influenced by the debate on the nature of angels. A consideration of the nature of angels is therefore at the heart of the book.

The problem which the scholastic thinkers had spent centuries of often fierce controversy in discussing was this: how is it that angels who are purely spiritual beings with no physical attributes whatsoever, can have a knowledge of the material world? For some modern theologians, questions like these, regarded as the equivalent of the "how many angels on the head of a pin"debates, are an embarrassing irrelevance. In 'The Vision in God', however, Desmond Connell insists that speculation about angels is philosophically and theologically important. He believes that they exist and that they play an active part in human affairs: "The Judeo-Christian tradition teaches that beyond the material creation to which man belongs by reason of his incarnate nature there exists a purely immaterial creation composed of a multitude of beings called angels ... Like man they were given the opportunity freely to decide between accepting or rejecting the Divine offer of friendship. Some accepted, and these are the blessed spirits who enjoy the beatific vision; some rebelled, and these are the fallen angels who are excluded forever. Both the blessed spirits and the fallen angels have intervened at decisive moments in the history of man's fall and redemption."

The subject of angels should not therefore be cast aside as a hangover from the dark ages. "Christian theology cannot neglect the study of angels. Moreover, in view of the distinction between the natural and the supernatural orders, and of the theological axiom that grace perfects nature without doing it violence it might be expected that Christian thinkers would discuss the natural condition of the angels, their natural capacities and activities. The explicit content of Revelation sheds little light upon questions of this kind, but to the speculative mind such reticence presents a challenge rather than an obstacle."

The problem which preoccupies much of 'The Vision in God' is: how do angels know things? Does God put the ideas directly into their minds, or do they learn from experience? "Either the angel acquired the (likeness of things outside of itself) by contact with material things themselves, or else (these likenesses) are infused into the angelic intellect by God ... The main difficulty against (the first solution) is that it seems to demand the impossible. The angels have neither bodies nor senses on which material things might act, and it does not seem that a material thing could act directly upon the immaterial angelic intellect. How then could (these likenesses) be derived from material things? But the (second) solution has difficulties of its own. The number of material things is endless. It seems then that each angel would require an infinite number of (likenesses)."

And the solution to this conundrum? God knows all things by contemplating himself. The angels are allowed to share in his contemplation of himself. "Just as God knows all things properly in virtue of one principle, his essence, so the angelic intellect can know a plurality of things through one principle, for the angelic intelligible species are as it were a kind of participation of the divine archetypal essence in the angelic intellect. Thus the peculiar perfection of the angelic species is attributed to a direct link with the divine archetypal ideas."

'The Vision in God' is Desmond Connell's major philosophical work, the material for his PhD and the basis for his reputation.Although he promises in the book to continue his work on Malebranche, he has not yet published a sequel to these researches. He has, however, continued to defend such doctrines as the existence and nature of angels against the onslaughts of modernising Catholic theologians who, in the wake of Vatican 2 and all its call for aggiornamento or "up-dating" of the Church, prefer to see them as myths or metaphors rather than as realities. For Desmond Connell, such things as angels and the virgin birth are not only true, they are scientific facts. It is not just that these dogmas should not be changed, it is that they cannot be changed. They are timeless and immutable.

The second Vatican Council came to a close in 1965, but it remains the central event in the life of the Catholic Church. On the interpretation of what happened in the Council hinges the whole power struggle between liberals and conservatives. On this essential question, the views of Des Connell coincide with those of another Catholic philosopher active in the 1960's: Karol Wojtyla, now known as Pope John Paul II. Dr Connell has published no remarks on the Council itself,but some of the fundamentals of his way of thinking are such as to preclude a liberal interpretation of what happened within it.

What is more, he made those fundamentals clear at the time, 1967 and 1968, when the tide within the Church was a liberal one,when Catholic theologians everywhere were "exploiting the insights of Vatican 2" in order to emphasise the new openings for change and development within Catholicism. Some Catholic thinkers, like Karol Wojtyla in Poland and Kevin McNamara in Ireland stressed that the changes attributed to the Council were "exaggerated"and that the whole process was really one of presenting the eternal dogmas in a more modern way rather than of introducing anything new. Without talking directly about the Council itself, Desmond Connell aligned himself with this current.

In 1967, just two years after the close of the Council, a British theologian, Professor Leslie Dewart, published a book called 'On the Future of Belief' which had, at the time, a considerable theological impact. The book was about Catholic dogma and the way it is formed. Taking his cue from Vatican 2 Dewart argued that an understanding of God and of the church's dogmas would have to be "drawn forth from contemporary experience". He attacked the Thomistic and scholastic philosophy of which Desmond Connell was a dedicated practitioner as being based on ancient experiences which contemporary man had outgrown and which he saw as "a primitive or infantile stage of development". He maintained that the idea of truth to which thinkers like Dr Connell adhered "attributes to truth an immutability incompatible with the genuine development of dogma". Stressing the "historical character of man, of truth, of dogma" he maintained that Catholic dogma "need no longer be understood as an essentially constant and substantially immutable object objectively presented to the Christian intellect". Instead, Dewart proposed a much greater role for the intelligence and faith of the individual believer.

Dewart's attack on scholastic philosophy stung Desmond Connell into the only public controversy of his entire career. He attacked Dewart at great length in three articles in the Maynooth-based Irish Theological Quarterly, accusing him of dangerously undermining the basis of the Catholic religion. Dewart maintained that our knowledge of things developed through the ages, and essentially, that we learn more as we go along. Connell replied that this was not the case, that man developed only by "living ever more perfectly" what he always was. Dewart maintained that it is human beings who create the meaning of any experience. Connell replied that it was God who created everything: "For the pure philosopher, this may be serious enough, but for the Christian theologian, it is surely critical when seen in the light of the doctrine of creation."

Dewart claimed that the truth of any Catholic dogma was about "the degree to which the development of consciousness actually occurs". Connell remarked that "According to this estimate, truth means essentially being up-to-date and error means living in the past ... This is to abolish the objective distinction between truth and error in favour of a historical relativism and subjectivism."So while Dewart suggested that a religious dogma which might be true for one historical period might need to be changed in another period, Desmond Connell insisted that truths were eternal and unchanging. Dewart saw the idea that the dogmas of the church were essentially completed with the Apostles as a "delicate issue". Connell replies bluntly that "With this we cannot agree." There is no delicate issue, only truth and error.

If the language of this debate is abstract and abstruse, its significance is not. If the truth cannot have changed from one period of history to the next, then Vatican 2 cannot have brought about any real change in the Church's dogmas, only a new way of presenting them: the position taken by the thinkers like Karol Wojtyla and Kevin McNamara. "For the Scholastics" says Des

Connell "the articles of faith ... derive their character ultimately from the fact that these judgements are made in consideration, not of their own intrinsic evidence, but of the truthfulness of God, who proposes for man's assent the object which they express. They constitute, therefore, a participation of man in the knowledge of God. The cultural form in which they express their object is accommodated to man's needs, but the object which they express is an object revealed by God."

The only role that the Catholic believer has is to accept the dogma that has been revealed, not to consider it for himself. "There is no other authentic relation of faith between man and God." New ways of putting forward the dogmas might be developed, but the dogmas themselves stay as they always have been. "The church has always been aware of the need to present her teaching under a diversity of cultural forms according to the various requirements of her audience ... But she has also believed that the truth of these different presentations of doctrine must be judged, not by their capacity to intensify the personal experience of the believer, but by their fidelity in expressing the content of divine revelation. On Professor Dewart's hypothesis, it is difficult to envisage the function of (the Church's) teaching authority. Would she not do better to let each one fend for himself? After all, what does it matter provided that personal faith flourishes? And in view of the fact that we all acknowledge the reality of faith in the various separated Christian churches, what becomes of the doctrinal differences that divide them?"

This dismissal of the idea of "letting each one fend for himself" is of crucial importance to Catholics in the Dublin diocese who might argue that on a matter like the use of contraceptives their conscience gives them the right to over-ride the "teaching authority" of the church. The idea of "individual conscience" is based on the belief that the individual Catholic has a personal relationship with God and that if this relationship allows them to contravene an article of the church's teaching, then they may do so. This whole idea is utterly and absolutely rejected by Desmond Connell. He not only denies that any believer, including himself, has a direct personal relationship with God, he denies that such a relationship is possible.

Whereas Leslie Dewart and many other Catholic theologians would see the essence of religion in the personal religious experience of the individual believer, Desmond Connell is dismissive of the importance of personal religious experience unless

44

it is fully in line with the church's teachings. "The truth of Christian faith" he says "is not a mere function of the intensity of a human religious experience: it is the truth of God dwelling in man through man's acceptance of the word of God. The truth of the conceptualisation of Christian faith is not to be measured in terms of intensity of the experience of faith, but in terms of its fidelity to that which God expresses to man in his word." In other words it is not the quality of the individual's faith which matters, but whether or not that faith is in accordance with the word of God as interpreted for the believer by the church.

The man who is now Archbishop of Dublin argues that direct experience of God by the believer is impossible: "For my own part, I have nothing but difficulty in finding a sense in which Christian belief might properly be called an experience. As I understand the term experience it refers to the immediate apprehension of some object, whether internal or external, which is directly present to the knowing subject. The object of faith as such, however, is not immediately apprehended in itself; it is apprehended only mediately, through the preaching of the Church, and guaranteed ultimately by the testimony of God. Moreover, the testimony of God is not immediately apprehended, but only mediately through signs whereby God manifests it."

What this means is that the individual Catholic cannot claim that their faith permits them to, for example, use contraceptives in contradiction to the church's teaching, because their faith only has value so long as it is in compliance with the church's teaching. The Catholic cannot claim an experience of God, only a knowledge of the "preaching of the Church". If the new archbishop remains faithful to a philosophical position which he regards as a scientific truth, there will be no room for his flock to claim that "I know God doesn't condemn me for taking the Pill".

Nor do these views bode well for the ecumenical movement that is so dear to the hearts of liberal Catholics. While there is nothing to suggest that the new archbishop will not enter into whole-hearted co-operation with the other Christian churches,his views on the unchanging nature of Catholic dogma preclude any possibility of compromise for the sake of Christian unity. And his attack on the idea of conscience and a personal relationship with God strikes at the heart of Protestantism in which such ideas are fundamental. Like the present Pope, he is equally committed to the centrality of the Virgin Mary in Christian faith, another stance which makes accommodation with Protestantism virtually impossible.

One of the few recent writings of Desmond Connell is a dissertation in Latin on the reasons why women should not be allowed to drive. The piece is tongue-in-cheek, but it is written in the style of a classical Thomist exposition, with six proofs of the proposition, each developed in its turn. It is hard not to see the joke as a reflection of his view on why women should not be allowed to become priests, an issue on which he feels so strongly that he described it last year as a matter of "life and death" for the Church.

Des Connell chose as the motto for his period as archbishop "secundum verbum tuum", the words of the Virgin Mary from St Luke's gospel - "Be it done according unto me according to thy word".He has a strong devotional attachment to the Virgin and in a 1984 address to a conference in Dublin praised Mary as "the faithful virgin who received the word of God and was obedient to it."

In his writing on the Virgin Mary, Desmond Connell again rejects any attempt to update the church dogma by seeing such notions as virgin births or miracles as myths designed to communicate the truth to a culture different from ours. "Myth" he says "is the device that draws the sting of the miraculous." To him miracles are realities, "the realities in and through which our faith is led to the manifestation of the grace bestowed in Christ." Those who oppose this view are not just on the other side of a theological controversy, holding views with which he profoundly disagrees. They are very close to being heretics. "To speak of myth may seem to accord with a contemporary outlook, but in reality it is close to the very early heresy which refused to accept the reality of the Incarnation ... To reduce miracle to myth is likewise to refuse to accept reality and to substitute appearance in its place."

Applying this belief in the absolute reality of miracles to the Virgin Birth, he sees it as not just a peripheral teaching of the church but as a central dogma for all Catholics, stressing "the fundamental nature of the revelation that God presents to our faith in the fruitful virginity of Mary." He places enormous importance on the idea of virginity and turns it from being an essentially female characteristic to being something which gets its highest expression in the male priesthood. His exalted idea of virginity becomes an argument as to why there can never be married priests or women priests.

Theologians anxious to enhance the role of women in the church have argued that the cult of virginity in the church has been tied up with a downgrading of sexuality and the role of women. The debate has also been important for those who argue that greater democracy in the church depends on married lay people being accorded the same theological status as the celibate clergy, which involves marriage and sexuality being seen as no less valid than virginity. Desmond Connell seems to go along with this argument by arguing that "Sometimes the mystery (of the Virgin Birth) is presented inadequately as if it involved the preservation of Mary's virginity in spite of her motherhood, as if virginity and motherhood were opposite realities which in her case were miraculously preserved from conflict. To view the mystery exclusively in this way is to tend to see it as a device by which God preserves the virgin from the taint of sexuality. But what is involved is something wholly positive: the raising of virginity itself to the perfection of fruitfulness."

He goes on immediately, however, to make it clear that virginity is something above and beyond sexuality, on a higher plane: "Sexuality is not a taint, but a reality of this world that is surpassed in the new reality revealed by fruitful virginity. Virginity is no longer sterility; by the action of God it has become a source of life." Mary is raised beyond the rest of humanity because she gives birth in a manner "that surpasses human generation". "Virginity has received a fruitfulness incomparably surpassing the fruitfulness of sexuality." And the highest possessor of this virginity which is exalted above sexuality is the "consecrated virgin" - the male priest. "The consecrated virgin is not the sterile one who has turned aside from the fruitfulness of marriage but the one into whose heart God's love has been poured and rendered fruitful in the service of God and his people." "There will" he goes on "always be a special relationship between consecrated virginity and ministry in the Church's life. For a priest has a particular association, in virtue of his call, with the fruitfulness of the Church." Behind the theological language, the meaning is clear: Virginity is of a higher order than sexuality: the priest is of a higher order than the lay person. The idea of equality within the church is impossible.

The point about Desmond Connell is not that he is personally opposed or uncongenial to change within the Church. It is that he believes deeply that such change is impossible. He sees his fundamental beliefs as matters of absolute fact and pursues their consequences with rigorous logic. As theologian Mary Condron puts it, "What he holds to is what has always been implicit in the Church's traditions. What is distinctive about him is that he has the guts to come out and say it."

Magill, February 1988

THE MORAL MONOPOLY

The People and the Theories Behind the Pro-Life Amendment Campaign.

It is a harsh rainy night on the Curragh as seventy-five people sit transfixed in the ballroom of Lumville House. "You don't have to look if you don't want to," the speaker had said. On the screen there is an image of primeval chaos; from the audience there are low groans. A tiny arm, a twisted half-formed leg, an umbilicus, another hand or foot, all strewn about the clumps of glistening raspberry-coloured blood and flesh. "This," she says "is the remains of a baby sucked out of the womb at ten weeks." For some, it is the incarnation of the words of John Paul II in Limerick: "to attack unborn life at any moment from its conception is to undermine the whole moral order..."

After the slide show and the speeches a man stands up to tell Loretto Browne "Ye're doing a great job, but what I want to know is this: I am against abortion and I am against it because of my religious belief, because of my Catholic faith. Why do ye put down ye'r religious belief?" "I wouldn't give up my faith for anything," she explains, but she points out that it is important for the Pro-Life Amendment Campaign not to seem sectarian. As the meeting ends queues of people gather round the table to enlist in the Society for the Protection of the Unborn Child.

Father Simon O'Byrne, author of "Civil Divorce for Catholics...Why Not?" and "Matt Talbot, Secular Franciscan", is preparing a new book on abortion. He leans across his desk at the Adam and Eve Counselling Centre in Merchant's Quay and begins: "I would like to state at this point, and I would like you to quote it anywhere you make reference to this, that I as a Franciscan OFM priest, I give full allegience to the teachings of the Church and to the Holy Father and to the bishop of the diocese, because there are priests who are for whatever reasons making statements which are or would seem to be contradictory of the statements of the Holy Father. For us, he is the one who has the supreme authority in this matter. There are no ifs and no buts. The mind of Christ and the role of the church instituted by Christ come before any state or any state law."

To Catholics who may be perplexed by the debate on the abortion referendum, Father O'Byrne offers "enlightenment": "You who say you follow Jesus Christ and are members of the one holy Catholic and apostolic church, you simply accept what the Holy Father says and what the bishop of the diocese teaches and do not allow yourselves to be confused by the opinions of others. Saint Paul warned us that the time would come when people would have itching ears and be seeking for new doctrines, and this is a time when there seems to be quite a rash of itching ears in our society."

Father O'Byrne believes that women become pregnant from "lack of faith and lack of due discretion". In twenty-six years as a priest he has never met any girl - "I'm not talking about a girl who is mentally retarded who is seduced" - who did not know that it is wrong to have sexual intercourse. "Ordinary modesty will dictate to a girl that bodily exposure of a certain nature is not the ordinary normal thing. They know it's wrong and they know it's seriously wrong and they know that it's the way in which children are conceived. They know it's wrong but they take the chance. But it's not mere knowledge that is necessary - the philosophy, the conviction, the faith in Christ, the dignity of the person."

He sees abortion as the result of the slackening of religious conviction. "What is happening in Ireland at the moment is a lessening of the sense of the supernatural, a lessening of lived Christianity. As freedom increases we're going to have more pregnancies outside marriage and then finding themselves in that situation and because there are facilities in this country and an organisation that is actually sending them and organising them to go to England and elsewhere girls will have more abortions. Like divorce, when abortion services are easily available, human nature being weak will take the easy way out."

Although it was not until 1869 that the Church decided to come out entirely against abortion from the moment of conception, Father O'Byrne does not believe that the earlier theological debates have any relevance now. "Some people have this idea that a little child has a child's soul. The soul does not occupy space; the soul is spiritual. Whether the person is ninety years of age or ninety seconds, the soul, when it leaves the body, is a full mature soul knowing all the mysteries and all the things that we don't know. The soul is created at the instant of conception. That is the teaching of the Church. That is what the Holy Father wants each and every one of us, which includes the priests and the sisters and the brothers and the laity, *all*, to accept.

49

"All life is equal because all deaths are the same. Whether it's through a spontaneous abortion or through an induced abortion, or shot in the North of Ireland or killed in the Falklands or dying of extreme old age at the age of a hundred and ten.

"There have been many discussions and treatises on this: when does the soul enter the body of the little person? From science we can never know. We can never know from science, and it's a question of the teaching of the Church. There is no positive way in which we can either in the scientific world or in the theological world say we can prove by seeing, by hearing, by some sort of physical measurement, that soul. But everything, the whole weight of proof, plus the tradition of the Church, plus the teaching of the Church, plus the command of the Church, is that it is there from the very instant of conception. And what were the difficulties with theologians and with others down through the centuries is not in actual fact an issue now. We thought that the world was flat and that if people went a certain distance from the shore they'd fall over the edge..."

In 1971 Mrs Valerie Riches was working as a medical social worker in a teaching hospital in London. She was also struggling with the difficult task of trying to bring up her adolescent children decently in a permissive society. When she heard that a new organisation was being set up "to stimulate an intelligent opposition to counter the insidious, persuasive propaganda that is undermining our society" she was delighted. She joined the Responsible Society immediately.

At the same time that Valerie Riches was taking this step, Dr John Bonar from Donegal was working in Oxford and campaigning within the medical profession against abortion; Dr Julia Vaughan was working in London and lobbying MPs for the repeal of the Abortion Act; Michael Hayes was lecturing in Norwich and had become chairman of the Norwich branch of the anti-abortion organisation Life. Now, John Bonar is Professor of Obstetrics and Gynaecology at Trinity College Dublin and one of the sponsors of the Pro-Life Amendment Campaign; Dr Julia Vaughan works in Mount Carmel Hospital and is the main spokesperson for the Pro-Life Amendment Campaign; and Michael Hayes is Professor of Mathematical Physics at UCD and Chairman of Life-Ireland.

"I saw the trauma and the actuality of abortion." Dr Julia Vaughan of the Catholic Doctors' Guild is sitting in the lounge of the Berkeley Court. "In the hospital where I worked abortions were being carried out and everybody right down to the porters were affected by it. They had not really been cognisant of the consequences of introducing abortion. If something is inherently wrong it must of necessity create problems."

"History has a habit of repeating itself," she says. "The protection of the law that everyone is pontificating about may prove totally inadequate." The 1861 Offences Against the Person Act, which prescribes a penalty of penal servitude for life for a woman who has an abortion, is the same law that was successfully challenged in Britain in 1938 by Dr Alec Bourne when he was acquited by a court, having aborted a fourteen-year-old girl who had been raped by a number of soldiers. "We have a constitution," says Dr Vaughan "and they have one in the United States. It is worth remembering that the right to life in the US was destroyed by a court judgement in 1973."

She believes that the life of the foetus is sacred from the moment of conception. "We are dealing here with life, something *we* cannot create." She believes that the IUD and the morning after pill are abortifacients. She does not regard the proposed amendment as sectarian. "The people who wrote the Constitution would never have envisaged any Irishman contemplating the taking of human life. It is unfortunate that the Protestant churches have come out against the amendment. Does pluralism mean that the state can condone wrong-doing? The unborn and helpless and unseen. You cannot do evil that good may result. Are people suggesting that for the sake of us all being happy together we should agree to people being killed?"

"Everything we do is all part of what we believe," says Professor Michael Hayes, chairman of Life-Ireland, which describes itself as "an inter-denominational, non-party political association". "I think one can't disassociate our actions from our beliefs. If we did we'd be running contrary to something basic there". Ireland, he says, is a more caring society towards children than Britain. "Occasionally you get a mother giving her child a belt on the bus, but that's very exceptional."

He does not think that any woman would agree to have an abortion without outside pressure. "It's unnatural, it doesn't stand to reason. But if something is available there is a tendency to use it. At some stage in their pregnancies mothers feel a bit uncomfortable. They need support and help, and in a way I suppose when the matter of abortion is mentioned it sounds like the solution, though indeed of course it isn't. Very often people regret it."

Father Simon O'Byrne regards Professor John Bonar as "a

51

leading Catholic gynaecologist and a man of deep faith and profound knowledge." In Oxford, John Bonar worked in a hospital where a thousand abortions a year were performed. "I've seen bags full of foetuses around twenty to twenty-six weeks being taken away to the incinerator, foetuses which probably with intensive care would have survived."

"The fertilised ovum contains the total genetic make-up of a new human life. Nothing is added to the fertilised ovum. It has the entire message. It's the same life from the fertilisation of the ovum until death. There is no change. It's very difficult on scientific grounds, on biological grounds, to make the cut-off point somewhere else. I'm not talking about ensoulment or the spirit. That's something for the theologians and the philosophers to discuss. All I'm talking about is biological life. The beginning is life. Man is man from the beginning."

If John Bonar was called to deal with a woman who had been raped he would make a personal decision as to what course of action would be appropriate. If he saw the woman within twenty four hours of the rape and he judged from the stage of her cycle that she had probably not yet ovulated and was therefore not yet pregnant, he would use the morning after pill to prevent her from conceiving. If he judged that the woman had already conceived, he would not treat her with the morning after pill. "I would hope that society would have enough trust in its doctors to deal with these exceptional cases...I don't believe in using hormones to induce abortion. I don't believe in using hormones to interfere with the process of implantation after fertilisation has occured. I would wish to have that decision left to me."

Professor John Bonar was one of the speakers at a meeting held in Ely House, headquarters of the Knights of Saint Columbanus, and chaired by Professor Eamon de Valera on 10 March 1980, around the time of the foundation of SPUC in Ireland. The meeting was on "The permissive society - its implications for Ireland", and the main speaker was Mrs Valerie Riches, now secretary of the Responsible Society of Britain. "In Britain today," she said "the family as an institution is under very serious attack indeed. The brunt of this attack comes from the media, which denigrates the family and presents the sick members of the community in a way which suggests that they are to be admired."

The bulk of Mrs Riches talk was given over to the explanation of her view of social change, which she felt it was vital for her Irish audience to understand. She spoke of "the network", a category which includes all those seeking liberal reforms. "In Britain there is a large network of interrelated organisations connected by a common personnel and ideology. It includes movements advocating family planning, abortion, sterilisation, sexual law reform, and the sex education of children... The network of organisations is fluid; new organisations are set up when it is thought expedient to campaign for further reform."

She explained that the network operates by infiltrating Government departments, the media and the women's organisations. Their most insidious activity is in regard to sex education in schools: "sex education is fertile ground for those who seek to change the traditional standards and mores of society. In Britain, the family planners, the abortionists and the homosexuals are clamouring to get into this field. They believe that our children should be taught not only about straight sex but also about perverse sexuality."

"I would like to relate," said Mrs Riches "what has happened in Britain so that you will understand and recognise the sequence that follows the all-important first step of legalising contraceptives." In the ascending scale of moral depravity she described the slide from contraception to abortion, to homosexual law reform. Manipulating all this movement of social change was the International Planned Parenthood Federation, whose members included the Irish Family Planning Association. Hardly anyone in Ireland had yet heard of IPPF. "The IPPF is not simply interested in the provision of family planning services in underdeveloped countries as the title indicates. It is also interested in what it describes as 'laws relating to the status of women', that is divorce, family laws, abortion, sex education, age of consent for birth control services and so on."

When Loretto Browne's mother told her about the inaugral meeting of SPUC in Ireland, she wasn't too pushed about going. She was on holidays from college at the time and had just finished exams. She did go to the meeting and gradually became more involved. "The more I see of the way people are being manipulated, the more I see of the untruth, particularly in the media, the more passionately concerned I have become to make sure that people know what's at stake - the fact that millions and millions of children are being torn apart day by day, and worse, that people like myself are being persuaded that this is civilised behaviour, that it is normal behaviour." She travels the country for SPUC, campaigning for the pro-life amendment, addressing an average of three meetings a week.

The turnout at Lumville House is very good for a wet Tuesday. Seventy-five people crowd the small ballroom. All, apart from two boys who have come in the hope of seeing some pictures of female genitalia, are quiet and serious. As the slides flash up on the screen, culminating with a black rubbish bag full of foetuses, everyone, including the boys, acknowledges the shock and the terror. "Now you can make up your own mind," says Loretto Browne, but her speech is just beginning.

"Agents of change are being imported to foist abortion on the Irish people," she says. "The Women's Right to Choose Group is a small group and a very pathetic group. Most of them have had abortions, and, were it not for the fact that they have each other for support, many of them would go to make up the statistics which show the high incidence of suicides among women who have had abortions."

She is quickly on to the subject of International Planned Parenthood. "When the Dublin Well Woman Centre was set up, Anne Connolly said there was no connection between contraception and abortion. There is a connection because the International Planned Parenthood Federation produced contraceptives in order to reduce the number of people giving birth. Margaret Sanger, who founded the IPPF, thought that only the elite should be allowed to reproduce."

Her view of the IPPF conspiracy follows exactly the pattern laid out by Valerie Riches of the Responsible Society. First, limited contraceptive services are introduced, then there is pressure for free access to contraception. This is coupled with sex education that teaches young people about the use of contraceptives. "If you vote for free access to contraception," she tells the audience "your kids will get them and use them even more because of no-holds-barred sex education. The more that use them the better for International Planned Parenthood. No contraceptive is one hundred per cent safe, so there are more unwanted pregnancies, and then the pressure is on for abortion." The Irish Family Planning Association, she says, is a full member of IPPF, and it has come out against the amendment to the constitution. "The amendment will prevent Anne Connolly from going full time into abortion."

One of the ways the abortion lobby works, she explains, is to argue on the basis of "soft cases". "Rape is very horrible, but most women who are raped don't conceive." She adds that "men that go in for rape are usually not fertile, they tend to be impotent." Even if a rape victim does become pregnant, it is no excuse for abortion. "A

54

woman who has been raped can have a washout. It may not be very successful but it can be tried." She looks around the room. "How many people here know how they were conceived? Do they know that they weren't conceived as a result of rape? That's worth pondering."

When she talks about IPPF, Loretto Browne refers to underlined portions of documents published by the Planned Parenthood Federation of America, the British Family Planning Association and the IPPF itself. These, she says, reveal the strategy for promoting contraception and abortion. "I would say that a lot of people who are in favour of what they would call comprehensive family planning services probably don't know anything about International Planned Parenthood. It's well known abroad. It's well known in America. It's well known in England, it's well known in Europe. It's not well known here simply because of the unfortunate stand taken by the NUJ which meant that people who knew a little of International Planned Parenthood couldn't make it public."

She believes that IPPF operates its plans for Ireland through the Irish Family Planning Association. "They work through the national family planning associations, and abortion on demand is one of the aims of International Planned Parenthood as written up in their literature. They operate by getting the social elite, as they call them, working through the media, working through voluntary associations, getting journalists and doctors on their side.

"Unlike trade unions or other pressure groups or political groups, national family planning associations tend either to be formed by the social elite or involve members of that social elite. I think we have seen this from the boost that the anti-amendment people have given their campaign by taking in people who would be well known in public life. There's Maureen Cairnduff, the socialite who holds a salon in Dublin every week. There are people like Dr Noel Browne. There are people like Professor Ivor Browne, and lots of other people. They don't know they've been got at. They should have more sense but they don't know they're being used."

She maintains that the media have been infiltrated. "From my analysis of International Planned Parenthood strategy, it's important to know that they do go for local control of the media in each country. As far as the media are concerned in this country, the NUJ, a British-based union, is the union to which a majority of Irish journalists belong. The majority of Irish journalists are not anti-life, but there is a strong section in that union who are actively supporting that union's pro-abortion policy. In key positions, editorial positions, producer positions in radio, television, newspapers, there is very definitely an anti-life stand."

Another part of the strategy is to influence "target groups". "The Council for the Status of Women is one group which is mentioned in Planned Parenthood of America literature. There's a five-year plan for Planned Parenthood of America, which is a member of International Planned Parenthood, and, as you know, the Irish Family Planning Association and other groups here would be a member of International Planned Parenthood through the European link. On page four it says 'On the world scene we take encouragement from world activity on population, food, and the status of women.'

"You are aware that in November 1980 the Council for the Status of Women hosted a women's day in the RDS, which I attended, and the discussion on contraception, abortion and sterilisation was completely controlled and manipulated by anti-life people, and there were a number of people there from abroad especially imported for the occasion." She spoke to someone in her own union, the Irish Nurses' Organisation which is affiliated to the Council for the Status of Women, about the IPPF stategy, but "she really didn't believe me."

Loretto Browne knows that the Internation Planned Parenthood Federation is responsible for the growing number of homosexuals in Ireland. "Margaret Sanger, the woman who started International Planned Parenthood, had a friend, Dr Havelock Ellis." Ellis, she says "was a bit of an oddball". "He intimated that all sexual relations, provided they weren't physically harmful, were quite acceptable, and that included sexual relations between people of the same sex."

Loretto Browne was at a meeting in Trinity College in October 1980 when a gay rights group offered support to the Women's Right to Choose Group. She knows that all the people in Ireland who say they are gay could not really be so. "Let's say that in the last couple of years in this country we have seen an unprecedented rise in the number of people who call themselves gay. By natural law we couldn't have that many misfits in society. And I don't mean misfits psychologically. They are - there's something wrong with people who think they are gay if they're not actually physically deformed. There couldn't be that many physically deformed people in society."

When Loretto Browne has finished speaking at Lumville House, she is followed by another speaker from the Pro-Life Amendment

56

Campaign. She is Mrs Bernadette Bonar, chairwoman of the Irish branch of the Responsible Society. The Responsible Society is affiliated to the Campaign, along with the National Association for the Ovulation Method, Muintir na Tire, the Irish Nurses' Organisation, the Irish Guild of Catholic Nurses, the Catholic doctors' Guild, the Catholic Guild of Pharmacists, the Congress of Catholic Secondary School Parents' Association, the Council of Social Concern (whose members include the Irish Family League, STOP and Youth Alert), the Catholic Young Men's Society of Ireland, and the CBS Parents' Federation.

Mrs Bonar is a pharmacist and a member of the Eastern Health Board. She warns the audience not to relax their vigilance in the campaign against abortion. "I know of one TD who has spoken out against abortion, and every week coming to his clinic there's a couple of seemingly respectable little women giving him sob stories about twelve-year-olds being raped and getting pregnant and the like." She attacks Dr David Nowlan, medical correspondent of the *Irish Times* and a member of the Central Council of IPPF, as "striking at the heart of journalism". She says the amendment campaign has "nothing to do with religion". "Anything you do down here you have to keep looking over your shoulder at the North. I think we should look after our own values first, and I come from a staunchly republican family myself."

"It is the leaders of society who cause crime, never the ordinary people. I know this campaign has the support of the ordinary people down the boreens, in the alleyways and down the backstreets." She explains the aims of the Responsible Society and finishes by warning parents who are sending their children to universities in Dublin. "My own daughter came home with this one day. It's the Trinity Students' Union handbook. As you can see, it's full of information on contraception, abortion, homosexuals, the Dublin Well Woman Centre. It's all here. It's as well that you know these things."

At the back of the room, on a table with anti-abortion literature and books with titles like "Population Growth: The Advantages", there is a pile of newsletters of the Irish branch of the Responsible Society. The newsletter has an item about SPOD (Sexual Problems of the Disabled):

"It is the promotion of mechanical sexual activity for its own sake, by all manner of artificial aids, with and without sexual partners....does this morbid over-emphasis on sex divorced from all other values really help any human person? Is he a better person or a happier one for learning all the techniques of sex and masturbation in an amoral context?"

Another item begins "SPOD and the Dublin Rape Crisis Centre are examples of how ultra-permissive forces can fasten on to what appears to be a compassionate or charitable cause." It goes on to describe how the Responsible Society and other groups fought against the renewal of the government grant to the Rape Crisis Centre in 1981. "It is our belief that in funding the Rape Crisis Centre the State is funding and lending respectability to promoters of abortion, even though the amount is small and it cannot be proved that the Rape Crisis centre as such is in any way connected with abortion or with abortion referral....After a long fight, the grant was paid to the Centre at the same rate as for 1980 which was well below the expectations of the Centre and thus represented a victory of sorts. It will be opposed again in 1982."

The Responsible Society's policy on illegitimacy is that "the removal of the so-called status of illegitimacy is an empty public relations gesture which does little of any value for the illegitimate child and at the same time serves to weaken the family unit founded on marriage, which is the cornerstone of Society."

Father Simon O'Byrne looks at his watch. A Swedish television crew is waiting outside to talk to him about morality in Ireland. He wishes to emphasise the point that the pro-life amendment is not a sectarian issue. "It's a pity that we make such an issue in the name of freedom" he says "when true freedom is only based on truth and truth comes from God and God revealed it through the prophets and Jesus Christ who was God. There has been no Protestant revelation, no Presbyterian revelation, no Baptist revelation. There is only one revelation. Truth is one and is for all. When and if the Christian churches become one as the Holy Father wishes, then all will accept the teachings of truth. I would encourage all who believe in Christ and all who respect the Holy Father Pope John Paul II, when the time comes, to go out and vote in favour of the amendment."

In Dublin, July 1982.

58

FIRE AND BRIMSTONE

Ivan Foster, erstwhile Commander of the Reverend Ian Paisley's Third Force, believes he may be living in the Last Days. An evangelical minister living in Fermanagh on the border with the Republic, he reads dark signs in his bible these days. "I turn to the New Testament where in the words of Christ, of Paul and Peter, very clear predictions are made regarding the End of the Age times. And it paints a picture of increasing lawlessness, and I recognise therefore that that which is prophesied in scripture is beginning to take place. Prophesying is a prediction, it's not a revelation that must happen and therefore we need not bother fighting it. It is merely a revelation to me that this is the trend that is going to take place and if you wish to avoid the consequences of such trends in your generation, you resist every move that leads towards that." Ivan Foster is Democratic Unionist Party member of the Northern Ireland Assembly for Fermanagh. In the Anglo-Irish agreement, as in the moral depravity all around him, he sees the signs of the apocalypse and hears the sound of marching feet.

Gregory Campbell, DUP Assemblyman from the Waterside area of what he always calls Londonderry, also takes his guide from his reading of the Bible. "I look at the scriptures and see in bible times what a people done where a government had forfeited the right to govern, where a people had been put in a position where they had no alternative but to take up arms, and I can only see that in those same scriptures that say you must love your neighbour, that having done all we can in a peaceable legitimate fashion, then there is no alternative but to resort to arms. I would look in the Old Testament where the children of Israel were put in a similar position. In the land where Pharaoh was king over them, they were told that there was no peaceable way out and the only option was to rise up and rebel and Moses led them out of Egypt though they were told by the Pharaoh that they were breaking his laws in doing so. They used physical breach of the laws in order to extricate themselves from the position that Pharaoh had gotten them into, but they only did that after Moses went to Pharaoh and said 'Let my people go.' What we're doing is the exact same thing. We will not go outside the law if we can do it inside the law, but at the end of the day we will take that option of breaking the law."

For Ivan Foster and Gregory Campbell, the signs are not only in the political dealings of the Anglo-Irish summit, but also in the wickedness of man which is courting Armageddon. Ivan Foster sees the breakdown of law and order in the Northern state as linked to moral depravity. "I would be very concerned for the future of any country that continues to liberalise and liberalise and liberalise. Because it is an indisputable fact that alongside recent developments, liberal trends, there has been an increasing social problem regarding law and order, in the home, in the marriage, in the schoolroom or just on the streets.

"It may be argued that there is no link, but I think there is a link. I recognise as a Protestant that if a Protestant loses his Protestantism, then he loses all motivation for opposing a United Ireland. It's immaterial to him who serves the Guinness as long as it's served. Under what flag doesn't matter, the political consequences of change don't matter. I see the danger of a population undermined by libertine trends that is gradually abolishing its spiritual heritage, its spiritual base, and since its spiritual base was always the source of its opposition to a United Ireland philosophy, that opposition will disappear.

"I think that we must take note of the fact that there is a great deal of coordination in all this. So I look for a coordinator. And as a conservative and orthodox Protestant I look to find the coordinator revealed to me in scripture - namely the power of Satan is at work."

One of the signs that the Reverend Foster sees that the end may be at hand, that it may be necessary to fight on to Armageddon, is that homosexuality has been legalised in Northern Ireland. "As a Protestant, and not a mere political Protestant, but as one who without apology believes the Bible, I come to portions of the scripture like Romans Chapter 1 where it indicates that society and mankind reaches the depths of decline and depravity when men turn from the natural use of women unto men. That's the pits, to use a modern phrase, you can go no lower. Paul at that stage speaks about the judgement of God coming upon a nation that does that. And whether we like it or don't like it, history indicates that when nations decline to those depths, they come to an end.

"It may have been their next door neighbour that put an end to them, and you may see no more to it than that, but I as a Christian see the moving of the neighbouring nation against the decadent nation as the judgement of God. Consequently I abhor the legalising of sodomy. I like that term, because if nothing else it annoys those who prefer to use modern euphemisms for what is nothing less than the sin which is associated with a city the doom of which is recorded in scripture."

Gregory Campbell shares this horror. "It's an evil, wicked, abhorrent practice. My opposition to that is based on the bible and also based on natural justice and I know many people who do not share my Protestant faith but who would share my opposition to homosexuality because they believe it is something which would corrupt society as a whole, and it is something so radically awful as to merit total and utter opposition. You're not even talking about something which is a run of the mill sexual practice but something which is totally and utterly depraved, and to me anyway the AIDS scare which is currently running through America is proof that homosexual practice is something which calls upon the curse of God. I would see homosexuality as something which merited the curse of God. There are others who are not homosexuals, and I'm not saying that everyone who has AIDS has got the curse of God on them, but the basis of the thing is that AIDS came about because of sexual contact between homosexuals. Now that to me is something which shows in a small way that there is more than just human opposition to homosexuality. In the bible there is only one sin which called down literal fire and brimstone from God and that wasn't murder, it wasn't theft, it was homosexuality."

Fire and brimstone, the Last Days, Armageddon, the images are deeply ingrained in the collective mind of the Democratic Unionist Party. Politically, Ivan Foster has a certain sympathy with the embattled whites of South Africa. "I have never studied the reasons for apartheid, but I have to say this: it must be a rather frightening thing when you have watched other African states given into the hands of races that to say the least have been catapulted into the twentieth century over the last few years, and if I were a white there I certainly would be very concerned about giving power into the hands of a majority and then to find that all that I had done, and my forefathers had done, would just be destroyed in tribal warfare and general, unsophisticated unintelligent attempts at governing the country."

Jim Wells is young and smooth, a Queen's graduate from the rich farming land of South Down, which he represents for the DUP in the Assembly. Now twenty-eight, he was in his last year at Queen's

61

when he was elected to Lisburn Council for his home district of Moira, where the large family farm is situated. He joined the DUP "because I like my politics cut and dried. If I'm in a party which favours the use of capital punishment for terrorists, I don't want to find as you find in the Official Unionist Party, that half the party doesn't agree with that policy. I like to know exactly where I stand."

Where Jim Wells stands is with the planter stock he came from. He believes in a separate Protestant race in Northern Ireland and in preserving the purity of that race. "I'm descended from settlers who came over from England and Scotland: my mother's side was Scottish and my father's side was English. There's been no intermarriage with Celts in the four centuries that we've been here. There's been no intermarriage in any section of the family over those centuries. And that's the same for many Protestant families. So we're direct descendants of mainland British residents, who carry British passports, who regard the Queen as their sovereign, and regard parliament as the sovereign body of this province, who regard themselves as an integral part of the United Kingdom, no different from Scotland or Wales. It's a fact, not something to be debated about. We don't feel British, we are British. That is what Southern people cannot grasp.

"They believe that because we live on the island of Ireland that we regard ourselves as Irish. Nothing could be further from the truth. I think we regard ourselves as more British than the British. I think we're the first to stand for the National Anthem and to show respect for the Queen, even more so than many mainland British subjects, many of whom have intermarried with Pakistanis and West Indians and allowed a dilution of their Britishness. That hasn't happened here and we remain militant British subjects. Here there's been very little intermarriage with immigrants or with native Irish. And mixed marriage is frowned upon; I only know of one mixed marriage in my experience. We at least have maintained our Britishness, even if other parts of Britain have wavered somewhat."

Jim Wells is one of those who does the frowning on mixed marriage. "I am totally opposed to mixed marriage. Of course I am. First of all because of the authoritarian attitude of the Roman Catholic church, which demands that the children must be brought up as Catholics, but secondly because I believe that anyone who indulges in a mixed marriage is betraying the Protestant cause. There's no excuse for mixed marriages in the North, not like in the south where the small number of Protestants means that, to be blunt, there's many a young man and young girl who wouldn't marry at all if they didn't marry a Roman Catholic. There's no problem such as that in the North where there are plenty of suitable Protestant partners. I would be against anything that would lead to a dilution of the Protestant population of this province."

Gregory Campbell has no mythology of the planter stock. In the Waterside there are no family farms, no tradition of property handed down over the generations. His legend of the Protestant race is different. "I think that the Ulster Protestant is a separate race of people from the rest of the island. In the general area that is now called Northern Ireland there has always been a separate and distinct type of people, code of ethics, morality. Everything about the way of life in the northern part of the island has been different to the southern part of the island, even before the plantation. There has always been a different race of people who inhabited the north. It happens at this stage to be the Protestant people who inhabit it. I have a different view from Gerry Adams as to how we came to inhabit this part of the island. He says we just came over as part of the plantation and usurped the Gaelic Catholics. I happen to believe that way before that, when the Picts came from central Europe, there were a people here who were different, who were usurped at that stage." For a working class Loyalist like Gregory Campbell the mythology of plantation becomes a mythology of dispossession.

But Gregory Campbell also wants to preserve the purity of the Protestant people and is against mixed marriages. "I make a distinction between integrated schooling and mixed marriages. I would be quite happy for my child to go to a school where Protestants and Catholics were taught together, but I would not be happy for my child to marry a Roman Catholic. I would be quite happy that the way I am bringing up my children would be sufficient to enable them to hold to their Protestantism no matter what their school environment would be. But that would be a different step from the child growing into a mature adult and then marrying a person who is not of the faith which she has been brought up to believe is the correct faith. If she chooses to do that, that's her affair, but it would not be with my blessing. I would hope that my children would grow up to be evangelical Protestants with a belief in the bible. That belief in the bible should preclude them from marrying someone who does not have the faith in the bible that they have. Also from a political point of view essentially what you are doing is asking a unionist to marry a nationalist and that is too much to ask."

That deep-seated Evangelical Protestantism is central to the DUP, and the fear of religious persecution is a large part of their fear of a United Ireland. Jim Wells sums up the objections to Catholicism: "We find much of Roman Catholic doctrine repugnant. I find repugnant the fact that any man has the right to forgive sins, that Christ can be recreated on the altar of the Mass Sunday after Sunday; that the Virgin Mary is regarded as a deity that can be prayed to, who can forgive sins and heal the sick and all that, that shrines which can supposedly move in Ballinspittle or wherever it is can delude thousands into believing that there are some magical powers. That is superstition of almost African tribal levels, which we find totally repugnant, and we just do not wish a situation to arise where we would find ourselves dominated by that type of system. If the priests can get twelve million pounds for an airport in the middle of a bog in Mayo, what can they not do to Protestants? Many Protestants would just have to get up and leave under those circumstances, they just wouldn't tolerate it.

"My view of the south is coloured by the experience of my relatives who refused to live in the south. My wife's mother was born in the Irish republic and all her folk lived in Cavan and Monaghan. And one hears the experiences that they went through as Protestants in the Irish republic, and the way that they were discriminated against overtly and covertly, and the way in which for instance they found it difficult to be educated except by nuns and priests and found it difficult to get teaching jobs because they couldn't speak Irish. Their civil liberties, in the form of birth control, divorce, that sort of thing, were controlled by a Catholic-dominated state, and many thousands of them were forced to come up here and live in Northern Ireland. When we see the way they were treated in the south, then that is enough to convince us that we don't want to go there. But could I say that even if the streets of Dublin were paved with gold and even if Ian Paisley were allowed to write the constitution, and if Dublin was a state flowing with milk and honey and motorways - which you don't have by the way - and all the paraphernalia of a western civilised society, we still wouldn't be interested."

That sense of a threat to Protestant faith by the southern state goes deep in the DUP. Jim Allister, the DUP's chief whip and former personal assistant to Ian Paisley, says that his own parents "had to move north out of the Irish republic where they were born." "I live in Fermanagh," says Ivan Foster. "I have always lived in Fermanagh. That's only a hop and a skip across the border. I know

64

the Protestants across the border. I know what they endured. Nothing visible, but what they had to put up with when they went to the mart, when they went to the shop, when they were looking for financial assistance. Whenever anyone else had a problem, they had ten problems. It was civilised behaviour, it may have forbade the use of the scythe and the billhook, but it didn't stop the manifestation of that animosity towards them. And I think it has been subdued so much over the last forty, fifty years because there was still a section of Ireland that had to be retaken, as it were, and it was no good pretending to be the best of friends while at the same time you were openly hammering the life out of Protestants. So the very existence of the Protestant majority in the north was the greatest guarantee that the Protestants in the south were at least given some degree of freedom. Even if that were not the case, you can't tell me that the people who are prepared to back murderers will not do me any harm if they get the chance.

"I have a dread in my heart at ever being under a Roman Catholic regime. I don't anticipate that if we were under a United Ireland tomorrow, that my house would be burned down and I'd be put out on the street and my children butchered, but without a shadow of a doubt, there are those who at this moment dislike me so much, not me as an individual but me as a being, that they are prepared to back those who would plan my murder and kill me, back them by their votes, back them by their support, back them by not turning them in. Have I not got grounds for fearing therefore a political change that will give greater freedom to those people who feel that way; freedom to express their opposition, to act out that opposition, act it out business-wise, social-wise, every way?"

Gregory Campbell, in another world might have been a socialist. The Waterside in Derry where he has always lived is no bastion of Loyalist privilege. "My parents weren't members of any political party, and paid no heed or interest to politics. My father was a serviceman in the navy. We were just the average Protestant family in Northern Ireland. The thing that pushed me into involvment in politics was the whole Civil Rights scenario, and the whole nationalist complaint and agitation that they were getting a raw deal. That was the clincher for me because I saw on the television screens and read in the papers where people like John Hume and the beginnings of the SDLP were agitating for Catholic rights, and at the same time I saw the type of community that John Hume was from and the type of living standards that they had, which were very similar to my own.

65

"Barry White's biography of John Hume makes great play of the fact that Hume was a working class Catholic, no bathroom, two up, two down, outside toilet. Well I had the exact same. I saw the nationalists were campaigning for better living conditions, jobs, voting rights, and yet everything that they were campaigning for, I hadn't got either. I hadn't got hot running water, I had to go outside to the toilet, I had all the disadvantages that the urban Catholic had, and yet they were campaigning as if it were an exclusive prerogative of Catholics to be discriminated against. I felt the exact same way.

"Obviously I thought about their deprivation and I thought about what kind of political structures there might be to bring about a better society, but there continued to be an attitude on their part that they were the only ones being discriminated against, and that I was part of the group that was discriminating against them. There seemed to be a continual diatribe against me, against people like me. We were first class citizens and these people were separated, were downtrodden and different. And it never seemed to get across to them that the people they were agitating against were in exactly the same position as them. Maybe in the early days there was a socialist ideology in the Civil Rights Movement, but it was always couched in terms of republicanism which obviously distanced me and people like me from it.

"I joined the Young Unionist Movement and I found myself campaigning for people that I was still socially opposed to. I found myself campaigning for people like Robin Chichester-Clarke, brother of the former Prime Minister, and to me that person was on a different social scale, a different planet. The guy was a highbrow Tory who cared very little if at all for working-class Protestant people, who were the people who were electing him. And gradually I moved over to the Protestant Unionist Party, which at that time, 1970-1971, was just changing over to the DUP."

Sammy Wilson, the DUP chairman of the Planning Committee of Belfast City Council, is also from a working-class background. "I've lived most of my life in East Belfast, which is perhaps in Belfast now the stomping ground for the DUP. It's a strongly traditional Loyalist area where there was a fair amount of social deprivation, far worse housing conditions even at present, and longer waiting lists for houses, than you have in West Belfast. I was attracted by the new dimension which the DUP introduced into Ulster politics and that was the radicalism which can be seen for instance in the kind of people who left here and went to form the

66

backbone of the American revolution, their dislike of the old establishment and the system. In the longer term it's the potential radicalism of the party which attracted me, representing as I do an area where there is terrible housing and other social problems."

He does not, however, like to be called a socialist. "I think it's one of the problems with those kind of labels in Northern Ireland that the constitutional question has really overridden other considerations. Socialism is, mainly because of the actions of the Labour Party, identified with republicanism. Socialism isn't a term that people use very often in Northern Ireland and yet if you look at the things that they believed and the ideas they would put forward, I suppose if they lived anywhere else they would be socialists. I would prefer, because of the stigma which attaches to socialism, the term radicalism rather than socialism.

"One of the problems of Irish history is that the concentration on the constitutional question by nationalists gave the excuse for not dealing with and not prioritising the social issues, which affected the Protestant people as much if not more in some cases, than they affected the Roman Catholic people."

With that view of the Protestant poverty, there is little sympathy in the DUP for talk of Catholic alienation. "Alienation?" says Jim Wells. "There's many who feel alienated all the way to the bank. Catholics in West Belfast have houses that would be the pride of Dublin and many of them have top jobs. How many Protestant barristers are there in Northern Ireland? Catholics have prospered and increased in numbers in Northern Ireland. They have retained their own educational system, the GAA gets more money for facilities from the oppressive British government than they get down south, in some cases they have their own hospitals, all funded by the state. I do accept that Roman Catholics feel that the old structure of Stormont did not give adequate expression to their viewpoint, and I am realistic enough to accept that there will be no return to a one-party majority rule state. But the SDLP have been given a veto on all new arrangements for devolved government and until that veto is removed they have no incentive to come to terms with the unionists."

The DUP is implacably opposed to any role whatsoever for the Irish government in the running of Northern Ireland. Even if that role is minor, "consultative" and cosmetic, they see it as the beginning of the end, the road to Armageddon. "While we're interested in the fine print of an agreement, and we will study it carefully, the fact that for the first time the Dublin government are going to be given an input in any way, that will be enough to trigger off all of our opposition, whatever the fine print," says Gregory Campbell. "If Tom King were to say to us, 'Look, we're only consulting Dublin about the colour of the lamp-posts,' that is sufficient for us to say that for the first time Dublin has a toe in the door. It's only a few months or a few years from advising us on the colour of the lamp-posts, to telling us what way we will conduct the traffic, to what way we will dress the police, to what way we will arm them. If Dublin is to have a say in any respect, if they are to have a say in that the Flags and Emblems Act is to be repealed, because Peter Barry and Garret FitzGerald have said it is offensive to nationalists and must be repealed, something that is regarded as small beer, then the British government will be sitting down and listening to the views of the Dublin government. Sovereignty is sovereignty. You either are sovereign over a part of a country or you are not. If Dublin has a consultative role, that is the beginning of the end. I would see the final day had arrived whereby Ulster had finally been sold, and we would have no other option but to exhaust the constitutional process and then proceed as quickly as possible to arming ourselves and to fighting.

"Let's not forget that Haughey is waiting in the wings and if FitzGerald were to put his toe in the door, Haughey will be coming through the door. Fianna Fail aren't going to be content with the colour of the lamp-posts or of the police uniforms or with the Flags and Emblems Act. They are going to demand a more meaningful role and subsequent summits will increase that role. What they are beginning is a process. John Hume calls it a healing process. Well, as far as we are concerned it is to open a wound, to fester the wound and to rub salt in the wound. We will find ourselves at the very end of the constitutional road and we will find ourselves in the very same position as Carson found himself in at Balmoral in 1912, where we will have to get every able-bodied man in Ulster armed as best we can, whether it is with guns or with sticks. Once the ink is dry and unionists acquiesce in any way to Dublin involvement, then we are finished."

"You don't give a consultative role if it doesn't mean anything," says Sammy Wilson. "Once that role is conceded nationalists on both sides of the border would want to work on it and develop it, and what might seem innocuous initially could be the embryo for a huge monster which would eventually gobble us up. Our case is this: that when it comes to the internal arrangements in this province, to the developing of powers, the government requires that there be widespread acceptance of any changes. Yet when it comes to a much more major constitutional change, that is giving an outside government a role in Northern Ireland, the government is not prepared to concede that it required the measurable widespread acceptance of this community."

According to Jim Allister, the DUP Chief Whip at the Assembly, unionists have a carefully planned strategy of opposition to the Anglo-Irish package. "If it gives a role to the Dublin government, it is unacceptable, no matter how innocuous it may seem. Assuming that that is the case, then we set ourselves on a course of seeking to undo that process. Our first bounden duty is to exhaust each and every constitutional and democratic facility we have. We may not have much confidence that we will achieve that end by these methods but we have the avenue of trying to thwart and destroy the agreement through parliament, and that can go out into the avenue of seeking to disrupt the parliament process, even to the nitty gritty of seeking to disrupt the government's timetable.

"Then there is our task of seeking to demonstrate that the community has rejected the agreement, through petitions, by-elections, a referendum, or whatever means we think appropriate. After that we begin the process of making the province ungovernable, both through learning the lessons of the 1974 Ulster Workers' strike and through pulling out of even lowly local government. The day Dublin civil servants arrive in any shape of form to administer this province, that is the day that we say 'Right, do it on your own, we're pulling out of every tier of government.'

"If we have done all that and we are still rejected, then they would have rendered me redundant as a politician, but they would not have rendered me redundant as an individual Loyalist, and then I would act in concert with hundreds of thousands of other individual Loyalists in arming ourselves. No self-respecting individual is going to do anything but resist. In those circumstances there are no lengths to which Ulster men would not go to stop it. None."

According to Gregory Campbell, the Loyalists, having obtained what they regard as a mandate in a referendum of by-elections, and having failed to stop Dublin involvement in Northern Ireland, would "say we must form ourselves into a provisional government; that provisional government must have a defence; and that defence must be armed. The Protestant people must be armed. That is my own personal view of how the situation lies ahead.

"In the setting up of a provisional government there would be so much community tension, that, well, I hesitate to use the words civil war, but there would be so much community tension that we would certainly have the kind of violence that we haven't seen since the early seventies. Even then it was contained to North Belfast, the Bogside, West Belfast, Armagh, Fermanagh, but in this instance the whole province would be embroiled. And there would be much more numerous deaths. That's the logical conclusion of what I'm saying. I realise that. I see that as going very near to the edge of the Protestant faith, of what I have held dear for twenty-five years. Obviously I'm not going to do that lightly, and it's not something that I would relish. But knowing Margaret Thatcher as we all do, as Arthur Scargill does, it's not likely that she's going to back down and we have to prepare ourselves for the inevitable.

"Dublin and London are slowly coming round to the position of blackmailing the Protestants, of saying 'you either have your country and you have your peace, and you have your guarantees or else the alternative is that you have civil war'. Now, given that option we will not have Dublin rule. We cannot have Dublin rule. And I know how terrible, now horrible, how awful the consequences of me going to the logical end of my argument are. But I will have to act in my community as a safeguard, as a safety valve, as somebody whom the community can use for letting off steam, and try and channel the paramilitary activities in the best way possible. And I will have to try and minimise the effect it will have on the country in the event of that type of Armageddon situation coming about.

"But I have to say that if these are the options, to have a greater degree of peace and stability than we have had and to have guarantees within the United Kingdom, if we let Dublin have a small role in a consultative way in Northern Ireland, or to have an opposition which will result in widespread violence, then I am going to be pushed into a position where I have to adopt the second role."

"Unionists are not spoiling for a fight and we are not itching for a civil war," says Sammy Wilson. "We've got to live in this country and I hope I have a long time to live in this country. Personally I would like to be as comfortable as possible and to live as long as possible. I don't want to be warring and fighting and living in a Lebanese type situation for the rest of my life. If I was sixty-five maybe I could tolerate if for a few years, but not when you're fairly young. So no one is going to embark on any course of action unless we're sure that there's a real threat. But regardless of how innocuous it looks in the immediate term we'll be asking what lies behind it. If it does give a toehold to the Irish government, then we'll be seeking by all political processes that are available to us to oppose it. Once that is exhausted, I think people will quite rightly say 'We've done our best, and no one has listened to us'. At that stage the role of the politician is going to change.

"I don't like bloodcurdling speeches, to be quite truthful. I don't like issuing bloodcurdling warnings, because we have to live amongst this, so I'll be quite careful in what I say. But all that I can say is that once we as a Unionist population feel that our future is under threat and that no one else is listening to us, and we've done all the political things we can do, there will be a turning to other methods. And my fear would be, and we've already seen this in small measure to some extent, that once that process starts, it's not the kind of thing you can turn on and off like a tap.

"Once you start along that road, people start to look to all of those they imagine to be enemies, for example among the nationalist community in Northern Ireland. People will say 'Well, they're the ones who've been harbouring the terrorists'. Large sections of the nationalist population would then be open to the kind of retaliatory action which years of frustration would bring out. I imagine the republic would be seen as the threat, the ones who are pushing the constitutional claim, and you're not too far away either, so people would say 'If we're suffering, you'll suffer'. How it all ends I wouldn't even want to start dreaming about.

"I would no longer be a politician in that kind of situation. People would have to opt as to whether they wanted to maintain some degree of input and control. I myself would look for a role in whatever extra-parliamentary actions were available. I wouldn't be a very good general, so I would hardly imagine that they would sign me up for that, but I'm sure there would be something I could do in a situation like that. I wouldn't relish it, but I would imagine there are other people and that's their forte. I can imagine that there are people from the border areas, political representatives who have been going to a funeral a week at times, who might not be as restrained as I would be."

One man from the border is Ivan Foster. As a minister, his theology does not prevent him from wielding a gun. "Modernism has equated Christanity with pacifism, which is a load of rubbish. It is useful to throw in here that title which is given to the Lord in the bible where it says of him that he is a man of war. These Anglo-Irish talks are entering a phase where it is very possible that the state will become a tyrant and say to me as a British citizen that I am going to lose a part of my citizenship because a foreign state is going to be given a role in the running of a part of the United Kingdom. It is a Presbyterian doctrine, ground out in the hard mill of the days of persecution in Scotland, that when the government, or the king as it then was, forsakes his lawful role and begins to enforce his will on the people contrary to the contract that exists between him and the people, then the king is no longer the lawful head of state, he has become a tyrant. And it is a Christian's duty to resist a tyrant.

"I would have no hesitation. I wouldn't be joining the army of Ulster as a chaplain. I would be joining it as Joe Bloggs, an ordinary foot soldier. I would not be infringing my conscience or the word of God, but acting in complete obedience to both. I would have no compunction, not in the least. I know how to use a gun. There's no good carrying a gun if you don't intend to use it. And if I am ambushed, I have one prayer: 'Lord, let him miss the first time.'"

Magill, November, 1985.

DEV'S PEOPLE

The nun, Mrs Gorman remembers, knew what she wanted. Mrs Gorman keeps the keys to de Valera's Cottage, the neat little house at Knockmore, just outside Bruree, that is now a shrine to the memory of the patriarch. The roses that used to grow outside the door have been taken up and replaced with traditional paving stones. The cooker has been taken out from the grate and replaced with a traditional open hearth, the old iron kettle hanging from its hook. The lino has been taken from the floor and replaced with traditional flagstones. The bareness of the walls is broken by a holy trinity: a statue of the Blessed Virgin, a print of Daniel O'Connell and an embroidered American eagle in a frame.

The nun, though, was not much interested in these downstairs rooms. She climbed the steep, narrow stairs that led to what was once Eamon de Valera's bedroom. The bed, Mrs Gorman warned her, might be a bit dusty. She didn't mind. She climbed up on de Valera's old iron bed and lay there, her black habit spread out against the pink mattress. She looked up at the whitewashed sloping sides of the ceiling or, perhaps, out the tiny square window at the small patch of ground where, in his boyhood, as he later told the Dail, young Eamon learned everything from "the spancelling of a goat to the milking of a cow". After a few minutes she got out of the bed, came down the stairs looking contented and left.

Up the road, in another of the neat villages that dot this gentle Limerick pastureland, there is a woman in her late thirties. "I'm married," she says, "but we've been separated for eight years. He went off his own way and I've looked after our two daughters. One of them's still in school, but the other's in London. I have a man who comes in to me a few times a week, but he's afraid to move in with me. Not that the priests bother you any more. I had one nasty experience a while back, when a mother and daughter, who I can tell you were doing all they wanted to do themselves but liked to complain about other people, put the priest on to me. But that didn't last long - there's so much going on around here now that they just don't bother any more. Still, as soon as my youngest one is reared,

I'm getting out."

The young man who works in the garage in Bruree and is going home to Kilmallock and then, maybe, out to Madonna's Nite Club in Charleville, knows all about leaving. "There used to be 10 of us would go out together every Saturday night. After this week, I'm the only one left. There's a whole street in Elephant and Castle, it's more Kilmallock than Kilmallock, if you know what I mean. Sure, there's all that history around here, but what difference does it make? The young people just aren't interested in politics."

Yet the past has its power around here, not least because the present keeps returning to it. At Knocklong, the railway station has closed and the bus just comes once a day. The maple-floored ballroom is closed up and the hotel no longer takes guests. There used to be traditional music a few years ago, played by an Australian couple and an Irishman, but the Australians went home. The Bord Failte traditional holiday cottages have been sold off. The days of turmoil when Bruree and Knocklong knew not one civil war but two - the big one when two thousand Republicans fought two thousand Free Staters for control of the Kilmallock Triangle, and the little one a year before when workers in both villages declared themselves Soviets and flew the red flag for a few days - are long gone.

What remains of those days is the de Valera museum in the old schoolhouse in Bruree. Here you can see the relics of a famous man's life: a headline copy book with the curling, punctilious handwriting - "Queen Victoria was born 24 May 1819." A jacket with a Fainne worked in thread on the label. Prizes won at sports meetings and War of Independence medals. Rosary beads, prayer books, spectacles, a walking stick. The old school desk with the carved initials "ED" that had to be deepened and enhanced before the museum was opened in 1972. And, more than these things, the words that de Valera spoke at an after-Mass meeting in Bruree in 1955 and that still remain in the hearts of many who live in and around the village: "The Irish language is the bond that keeps our people together throughout the centuries, and enabled them to resist all the efforts to make them English. It would be useful to us that way today, when we have poured in upon us, from every direction, influences which are contrary to the traditional views and hopes of our people. It is on the character of our people that this nation will be built, and the character consists of very simple things: earnestness in our work, honesty and truthfulness."

In the Deerpark Hotel in Charleville, they have their own little exhibition: a print of the scene in the GPO in 1916 beside a photograph of the shopping centre in Charleville, Australia.

*

The first time, a helicopter ever landed at Bruree was on a Sunday evening in July, 1966. Not one but two of the great whirling machines descended from a clear blue sky on to Knockmore Hill, one carrying the President of the Republic the other containing his body-guards. For Lorcain O Maonaigh, a local farmer and veteran member of the Eamon de Valera Cumann of Fianna Fail, it was a day to remember. His daughter Maire was four at the time and he arranged for her to present the President with a bunch of flowers.

Dev, he says, was both pleased and amazed that a little girl from Bruree would be able to speak such good Irish as Maire could. The memory is a source of great pride to him, a part of his firm belief that "apart from politics altogether, Dev was, a great man, a wonderful type of person." It is one of the things that has kept him loyal to Fianna Fail through all the decades of change.

The other thing is the memory of an empty house. Lorcain was a young man when his uncle took him to see the house over the Cork border. It was in the house that a brother of Lorcain's mother was killed along with three other men during the Tan War. The men were having a meeting of the local IRA Brigade when the Tans attacked and shot them out of hand. One of those killed was a young man who had just built the house and was waiting to move into it with his bride-to-be. The house was never lived in again, and it stood there for decades, an admonition and a call-to-arms.

Lorcain isn't sure when he joined Fianna Fail, since it seemed that he was always in the party. After the Civil War, you always knew which side you had been on, and his family's side was staunchly Republican. "It wasn't that there was much bitterness or enmity round here, it was just that there was a different sort of relationship. The Fianna Fail fellas knew each other very well, and the other crowd knew each other very well and there'd be a different sort of a handshake if you met on the road, that sort of a way." A man who lived at the end of their boreen used to take Lorcain to Limerick every time that Dev was in town. "I grew up with all those people, and I never changed."

That loyalty, though, hasn't been easy. He watched the rise of the Men in Mohair Suits from the Sixties onwards with distinct unease. "I wouldn't go along with 'em now. These men came from a different generation and they probably have a different education, but they'd want to look back to their roots, like. I don't see why they're yapping so much about republicanism if they're short of the whole picture. In the cities, people are different and they come more under outside pressures. You have writers and third-level students and intellectuals and those, and they mean great, but it doesn't all work out either. Charlie's had the divil's own luck - people have come to accept that they have to tighten their belts but you hear of the politicians then going on junkets. I do think that when people move into positions of power, they're often inclined to forget what put them there. I think de Valera was one of the few men who didn't ever forget his roots.

"When I was younger I would go canvassing, but now a lot of the things I thought were important, our people in the party don't bother with. Dev now, when he'd talk, the Irish language would have a priority. He'd always begin his speeches in Irish and go along a good way, and then turn to English. But the people now, I don't know are they Irish or English. It isn't for me to say, I suppose, times are changing.

"Until we get proud of ourselves again, I can't see us doing anything. I see ads on the television and they're advertising books on nature and they're saying 'the Book of the British Countryside'. That gets me. A lot of our TDs are decent enough people, but they don't seem to think about things. If we want independence we'll have to do something about it, and if not, we might as well sink back into the British world."

He is not convinced that the party is as serious about a United Ireland as it was in Dev's time. "I've a lot of regard for Charlie, but Charlie, too, is not altogether a disciple of de Valera's republicanism. A very, very able man, now, and a very human man, but I don't know has Charlie the right mix either. This Anglo-Irish Agreement, for instance, is so vague that both Charlie and Maggie can get something out of it. 'Tis just about better than nothing. A heap of words." He feels that the violence of the Provisional IRA was inevitable because of the way the Catholics in the North were treated and he had a great deal of sympathy for the H-Block hunger strikers: "There's a thing about it - you might not agree with these people, but they're your own people, no matter what.

"I think Dev would be fairly disappointed with the party now. But 'tis like Daniel O'Connell. He was regarded as the leader of the nationalist opinion, but the people who came after him didn't think that at all. I suppose you have to live in your own times. If you have a spade and a shovel and no tractor, you have to work with the spade and shovel."

76

The image of a man on horseback riding into Bruree playing the fiddle is one that has stayed with Mainchin Seoighe from his childhood. Fiddling away furiously, the horse being led through the village, the whole thing lit by the light of candles in the windows. It was a victory parade, a celebration of Fianna Fail's triumph in the 1932 election. He had seen de Valera for the first time a few months previously in Kilmallock. "He came from Newcastle West. There was a great turn-out, a torchlight procession and all the rest of it. I was too young to remember a word of what he said, of course, but the thing that struck me was I thought he spoke exactly as his uncle here in Bruree, Pat Coll, spoke. I would have sworn that it was Pat Coll speaking."

Pat Coll and Mainchin's mother were neighbours, and later, after he had assumed power, Dev would call sometimes to see her. In 1965, Mainchin spent a day with Dev, taking him around all of the old places. They talked about schooldays, about the pitched battles that the boys from Ballynaught used to fight against the boys from Tankardstown on their way home, about Montecarlo Bergin who got his name from singing "The Man who Broke the Bank at Montecarlo" and used to travel the countryside for Foxy Pat Coll, selling tea from a pony and trap.

Mainchin remains devoted to Dev, is the curator of the de Valera Museum and has written poems in honour of his hero, poems like "The Man From Bruree":

When you honour in song and in story
The men who at Easter uprose,
Who struck for the freedom of Ireland,
And faced the full might of their foes -
Oh, remember the man from Bruree, boys,
De Valera who answered the call,
He fought in the thick of the battle,
And was last to surrender of all.

Mainchin, too, thinks that Dev might be disappointed at the way both party politics and Irish society have gone. "Dev was prepared to accept change all right, but I'd say he'd be disappointed at the same time. He'd be somewhat stronger nationally than political leaders are inclined to think now. I think he'd take a firmer stand with Britain than any one of our leaders would now. He would have been pleased at the standard of living and of education that we have now, but I don't know about social change and all these things that

77

are being discussed now.

"Materialism, the consumer society, wouldn't be his ideal. You see when I was growing up, people round here wouldn't have thought anything strange about comely maidens and all that. It seems to the young people now that that doesn't make sense. But the older people would still believe in the moral order that Dev would have wanted. Society is so open now, with television and media and that, and young people are immature. There certainly seems to be a deviation from old standards. I grew up in the hungry Thirties and the isolation and, I suppose, insulation of the war years. Money was scarce, and we had none of the luxuries or amenities of modern life, but people were happier, certainly more contented than they are now. With advertising and everything now, young people's aims are set too high."

Politics in Bruree is more about getting the vote out than it is about persuading people to vote the right way. Persuasion has little to do with a political landscape whose contours were set down nearly 70 years ago. Padraig O Liathain, another long-standing member of the Fianna Fail Cumann in Bruree, says that you can still point to each household in the area and say how they will vote in an election. "Even to the present day, you'd know the families. Such a family is Fine Gael and such a family is Fianna Fail. I have never known families to change their allegiance, even going back to their grandfathers. The families are still loyal to the parties that their ancestors and forebears fought for. You can estimate the vote, and in a general election, you wouldn't be out much. You wouldn't hit it head on, but you'd be within a couple of per cent anyway."

Even getting the vote out isn't as much of a task as it used to be. "In the early years, transport wasn't as plentiful and that was the problem. Up to the 1960s, there'd be two cars out in this area operating a shuttle service all day long. The Lemass era changed all that - now there's only one or two people who don't have their own transport."

Padraig's mother's people were very active in the War of Independence and when he was 16 and wandered into a Fianna Fail Cumann meeting by accident, he joined up on the spot. That was 30 years ago. "Dev's first cousin, Mrs Maher, taught me at school, and we'd been hearing of Dev, little stories about him, old people that he knew. His name was a household word. There was fierce loyalty to Dev. No matter what Dev did or what he said, didn't matter. He was right, always right. It was never questioned. Now everything is questioned. Dev led and everyone followed. Nowadays, even if

78

you're a party supporter, you question what the party are doing."

His own period of questioning was when Fianna Fail was led by Jack Lynch. "I have strong feelings on the North, and they'd be very traditionalist. I don't think unity will come overnight - it will be step by step, and I think the Anglo-Irish Agreement is only a tiny step on the road to unity, but come it must. I think the party did lose the nationalism for a while during the Sixties and early Seventies, they did stray a bit, but I think since Charlie became leader they have come back a little bit again."

He is, he says, "against violence and murder", but "I wouldn't isolate the IRA and say that the IRA alone are commiting those atrocities - the British Army is doing it too, along with the militant Unionists. There's no easy answer. I would like to see Sinn Fein brought back into the political process, and I wouldn't support Section 31 either. It's a crazy situation, I think that if they have something to say, let them say it, and let people decide."

Like all of the Fianna Fail Cumann in Bruree, Padraig was against divorce, but he thinks it might come in a United Ireland. "Maybe when talks are held on the unification of the country, maybe then that would be the time to make allowances." But he doesn't believe social attitudes have changed around Bruree, anyway: "Moral standards are the same as they have always been. We'd be leading a different kind of life from cities and towns. In a rural area, everyone knows everything about everyone else. You can't be a Jekll and Hyde character. No matter what you do, it's common knowledge. That helps to keep people on the straight and narrow."

Next Friday, as he has done for each of the past 25 years, Padraig will be heading for the Ard Fheis in Dublin, with at least one or two members of his family. "At first, it was in the Mansion House, where the crowds were smaller and the atmosphere was more intimate. But even now you make a lot of friends there, you meet the same people year after year - it's more a social event than anything, with a lot of fringe happenings and functions. It's more a holiday weekend than a political event - I have an aunt in Blanchardstown and we stay there. I would go to some sessions of the Ard Fheis, but certainly not them all. I'd always go on a Saturday night for the leader's speech, of course. But most of the time would be spent going round in the vicinity of the RDS - the Burlington or Jury's or the social events in the hall itself."

Whatever happens this year for Padraig it is unlikely to match the year in the mid-Sixties when he was up for the Ard Fheis. He called to Aras an Uachtarain to ask if he could leave a photograph for Dev

79

to sign. "I just called to the gate of the Aras, no appointment or nothing. My mother was with me and my five year old son. I told the guard at the gate my business. He rang the house. Dev told the man to let us on in. We were ushered into the waiting room. Then we went into the study and sat opposite him. He spoke a lot about Bruree, families that he knew, trees and bushes that he remembered, the countryside and the simple life of the people."

This year, at the Ard Fheis, Padraig will be near to the building site which he will not recognise. On it the most expensive group of houses to be built in Dublin this year - set to cost between £275,000 and £300,000 each - are being erected. The site is the former home at Cross Avenue of the Man from Bruree, Eamon de Valera.

The Irish Times, Feburary, 1989.

B. AMERICAN DREAMS

LAND BEYOND THE WAVES:
IRELAND AND AMERICA

In the village church of Asdee, on that long stretch of north Kerry that lies between the Atlantic coastline and the great flat estuary of the Shannon River, Father Ferris turned from the altar to his congregation, his arms held wide apart to summon their attention. "In nomine patri et fili et spiritus sancti" intoned the parish priest as his right hand ambled across his chest to complete the sign of the cross. He paused to look down over his congregation, the men with folded caps clutched before them, the women's heads covered with scarves and mantillas. "My dear people, today's Mass is offered for the repose of the souls of Frank and Jesse James who died in America. Let us pray silently for their souls and the souls of all the faithful departed."

They closed their eyes, heads bowed, and thought as they murmured silent Hail Marys, of the souls of the ragged desperadoes leading their band of outlaws across the ghostly Montana range, in frantic pursuit of the American Dream. The mythical images came easily to the inner eye, given life and form twenty years earlier by Tyrone Power and Henry Fonda in the film *Jesse James*: Jesse shot in the back as he nailed a simple icon of the Virgin Mary to the cabin wall. These images of American mythology had a special home in Asdee: had they not been cradled in Ireland? Frank and Jesse were more than distant legends. They were also the boys from the next parish.

If you stand for long enough on the western coastline, watching the powerful Atlantic breakers, someone, sooner or later, is bound to take your elbow, and searching the horizon with a look of consequence, say "The next parish is America." The grandfather of Jesse James, like the millions before and since, left his Asdee home (where his relatives remained until recently) for America. 1847, the year Jesse was born in Clay County, Montana, was black '47 for his cousins in Asdee. It was the worst year of the Great Irish Famine which was to stamp the life of rural Ireland for a century. That same year Henry Ford's grandfather left County Cork.

In Asdee they kept Jesse's legend alive in their hearts, an image of

82

freedom, independence and money. Every year until 1959 Father Ferris said a memorial Mass in honour of the James Boys, and the surviving members of the Irish branch of the family, along with their neighbours, went to pray. The one holy, Catholic and apostolic church enacted its most sacred ritual in tribute to the abiding power in Ireland of the images and icons of the American myth. The James family of Asdee had always been known as horsebreakers; even, it was whispered, as horsethieves.

The iconography of America had the deepest and most intimate of connections with the West of Ireland. "Ireland," John Fitzgerald Kennedy said, on his visit to his Irish cousins in 1963, "has only one export, and that is people." The American Wake marked the transition, not from this world to the next, but from the Old World to the New. It was celebrated through two centuries in nearly every household in Ireland as the Great West opened its arms to the downtrodden masses. From Galway, New York; Killarney, West Virginia; Dublin, New Hampshire; Kilkenny, Minnesota; and from Shamrock, Texas the emigrants sent home money, the images of success, photographs of gleaming white houses, glistening black cars and gorgeous white children. They sent home a dream, an aspiration, as finally they would send home the icons of success to clothe that dream.

In the West of Ireland the American symbols now lie easily against the Irish landscape. The greatest of Irish-American inventions, the mass-produced motor-car conjured up by the exiled Corkman Henry Ford, seems almost an organic element. Indeed it has eventually insinuated itself into the topography of the west. Horses tethered at the side of the street in Westport or in Ballinasloe may evoke the heyday of Dodge City, but they do not seem out of place. The music which now dominates the dancehalls is the uniquely Irish version of American Country and Western. It is after all only Irish traditional music transported, packaged and re-exported. Only in the excesses of Hacienda Gothic, the building in the rain-drenched hills of West Mayo of bungalows meant for the sun-baked plains of southern California, does the confusion of cultures amount to a clash.

During the last century the Irish language under the pressure of emigration, practically disappeared as a vernacular. With it went the link in words and imagery to the Gaelic past. Victorian intellectuals, most of them urban, many of them from Protestant ascendancy stock, re-invented a Gaelic peasant imagery in their salons and libraries. By the time Ireland achieved its political independence in

83

1922, the images by which its very reason to exist was defined were already losing their power. Having achieved official national sanction, their actual connection to any kind of economic reality was becoming more transparently tenuous. A photographer touring the West of Ireland in the 1930s would have seen the sacred icons - the thatched cottages and the round towers, asses harnessed to the carts loaded with creels of turf, the pipes and the fiddles, the old women in shawls. However he would also have seen the emptiness, sensed the flow of the haemorrhage of people who took to the boats as refugees from the bitter poverty, stagnation and despair. The images that filled the photographer's frame then were the images of a dying world. They were also the only proof of Ireland's official sense of independent identity and they would be clung to with a ferocious tenacity for decades to come.

Who else to be the high priest of this mystical vision of Ireland but a man born in America? Eamon de Valera was born in the New York Nursery and Child's Hospital on Lexington Avenue but his mother, anxious to re-marry after his father's death, sent him home to County Limerick. There he attached himself to Ireland as a new mother, surpassing all others in offering proof of his Irishness. "Whenever I wanted to know what the Irish people wanted," he could say in 1921 with absolute sincerity, "I had only to examine my own heart." What he saw when he examined his heart became what the Irish people wanted, since he directed their destinies for four decades, as revolutionary, diehard oppositionist and Taoiseach. While those who could not live on imagery alone were taking the emigrant ship, de Valera was perfecting his vision of Ireland, shaping up to pronounce the ideals which the people of the countryside (the only Ireland that mattered to de Valera) were to live, and be inhabited, by. On St. Patrick's Day 1943 de Valera addressed the nation and expressed, more powerfully than ever before, the vision which had animated the struggle for national independence. "That Ireland which we dreamed of would be the home of a people who valued material wealth only as the basis of right living, of a people who were satisfied with frugal comfort and devoted their leisure to the things of the spirit - a land whose countryside would be bright with cosy homesteads, whose fields and villages would be joyous with the sounds of industry, with the romping of sturdy children, the contests of athletic youths and the laughter of comely maidens, whose firesides would be the forums for the serene wisdom of old age. It would, in a word, be the home of a people living the life that God desires that man should live."

84

The measured gravity of his voice, as he interpreted the desires of God to the Irish people, was some kind of balm to the pain of subsistence living, the economic inability to marry, and the sorrow of separation from the exiled.

And through all of this America was waiting, lurking beyond the harsh waters of the Atlantic with its silent promises of success. Its heroes flickered on the silver screen or wrestled with each other across the pages of the cheap cowboy novels which replaced the Irish books banned by the Censorship Board, on the library shelves. The envelopes full of dollars arriving from the brothers and sisters in Boston and New York were proof enough of the efficacy of America's myths and dreams. When de Valera uttered his Utopian vision, 25,000 Irish men and women, mostly from his sanctified countryside, were leaving the country every year, a figure that would continue to increase for the next two decades.

While the culture which nourished de Valera's vision of Ireland was being whittled away, his other great driving force, puritanical Catholicism, hastened its demise. Whatever was spontaneous in the social life of the countryside had to be contained and ordered; otherwise it was "an occasion of sin". The crossroads dances held on summer evenings in every part of the Irish countryside kept alive many of the social customs which de Valera valued, and kept Irish traditional music in the mainstream of popular entertainment. But the dances were feared by the clergy for their open invitation to sexual contact.

Two years after de Valera assumed power his government introduced the Public Dance Halls Act of 1935, a momentous piece of legislation for the cultural life of rural Ireland. It sought to regulate dances by making it necessary to obtain a licence to hold them. The intention was to curb the country dances held in houses or at crossroads and, above all, to make public entertainment of this kind more amenable to supervision, particularly from the clergy. The Act created the boom in the building of rural dancehalls. It also created a financial boom for the small country businessmen who allied themselves to de Valera's party Fianna Fail. For the first time in rural Ireland, music became a business, dancing a saleable commodity. The seeds of the Irish Country 'n' Western industry were sown. To this day there is an indisoluble link between that industry and Fianna Fail. A senior minister in recent Fianna Fail governments, Albert Reynolds, owned a large chain of rural ballrooms and, while he was minister in charge of telecommunications, appeared on television in a cowboy suit and

85

stetson singing *Put Your Sweet Lips A Little Closer To The Phone.*
The leading Country 'n'Western DJ in Ireland, Paschal Mooney, is a
member of the party's national executive. One of the biggest
Country promoters, Donie Cassidy is also a Fianna Fail Senator.

In the dancehalls both sexuality and music were muted, tamed and
controlled. The softer, smoother, more palatable and more saleable
sounds that were crossing the Atlantic could be packaged with the
exile's nostalgia and sentimentality. The timeless interplay of the
sexes could be reduced to a stilted ritual of selection and
postponement, the weekly combat of lust and economics, a ritual
both lucrative and conducive to salvation.

For all de Valera's sacerdotal recitations of his sacred images, his
Ireland was, by the time he retired to the ceremonial office of
President in 1959, the saddest of ruins, on the verge of complete
economic collapse. In the West of Ireland abandoned houses were
more common than inhabited ones, as emigration continued to soar.
There was no choice but to dismantle the economic barriers which
had kept de Valera's Ireland isolated from the world and the new
Taoiseach Sean Lemass had already begun to do so. The First
Programme for Economic Expansion was set in motion. The tariffs
against foreign trade were dismantled and Ireland threw its arms
open to American capital, looking to the west, where dreams of
work and money and success had always seemed to come true,
while the native businessmen had provided little or nothing.

When he moved over, de Valera left Ireland looking almost
exactly as he had found it. The horse and cart was still an everyday
sight in the 1950s. Except for the new housing estates in Dublin,
there had been little building. Shops, pubs, hotels and dancehalls
were the same: the high tide of chrome, neon and plastic had yet to
wash over the small towns, trailing new images of prosperity in its
wake. A man could wear his father's drab dark suit and not look out
of fashion.

The horse fairs which today are either rugged survivors, clinging
on to the traces of a vanished society, or revived for their colour and
sporting interest, still had a real economic function. In 1960 there
were only 4,100 tractors in use in the western province of
Connaught (43,700 in the country as a whole) compared to 39,300
horses used for farming (176,100 in the country as a whole). By
1975 Connaught had nearly 20,000 tractors and only 12,000 horses
working its farms. With the steady decline of the small-scale farmer,
the horse would become an emblem, a symbol of a way of life
rather than an economic entity in its own right.

If de Valera had sustained the Irish countryside through its bitter inwardness and poverty with his own ascetic iconography, a new symbolism would need to be forged to express the confidence, the acquisitiveness, and the unashamed display of the magnificence of money, that would inspire economic growth. In the glorious summer of 1963 a new father came down from the skies. De Valera went to Dublin airport to pass his mantle to the man he hailed as the Chief of "the great Republic of the West". The new father-figure was virile, sexual, rich and urbane, awesome in his contrast to de Valera, the dry, lean bird of prey. "My friends," said John Fitzgerald Kennedy, "Ireland's hour has come."

The new Playboy of the Western Republic, the apotheosis of the returned Yank, Kennedy personified the flowering ambitions of a new Ireland in which, suddenly, everything was possible. Driving round the country he embodied the lure of America. The great thing was that this was our own America, not foreign and threatening but Irish, Catholic and clean. He was the boy from the next parish who hadn't forgotten his country cousins when the big time struck.

At each stop he made, during every public oration, he would look up as he accepted the Freedom of Cork or thanked the Mayor of Limerick for her warm welcome, and ask the crowd "Does anyone here have relations in America? Can you raise your hands please?" And a sea of arms would ascend in aspiration towards him, each a pleading voice to say that its owner, whether he had American relations or not, wished to be included in the great communion of success. They reached for the hem of his garment, to feel the seductive cut of the American Dream. Every hand raised towards him was a cry of hope, a cry against the grinding despair of Irish life. Every hand was a hand that would sweep away the deadening vista of unfulfilled promises that was the history of independent Ireland. And Kennedy would smile a coy smile and say "My goodness I never knew there were so many of us over there" and move on to the same trick in another town.

"We have seen," said the Mayor of Limerick in her address of welcome for JFK "the introduction to Ireland of a new type of American, who is taking his place in our civic and social life. We trust that you will use your influence to send many more industrialists like them." In the coming years her prayers would be answered, as Ireland was transformed by massive grants and tax-free benefits from the Land of Saints and Scholars to The Most Profitable Location in Europe for American Industry.

Kennedy was worshipped in Ireland with a religious fervour in the garish triptychs, sold in the souvenir shops and hung in cottages all over the country, which depicted JFK, flanked on one side by his murdered brother Robert, and on the other by a portrait of Pope John XXIII whose Second Vatican Council had come just in time to free the Irish from the rigours of rigid Catholicism.

No one knows much about Bill Curtis, except that he was American, that he wanted to build a car, and that he wanted to build it in Ireland. In 1959, just as de Valera was retiring, Bill Curtis, after negotiations and deals of various sorts, obtained premises in Castleblayney, County Monaghan and started to build the Shamrock. The Shamrock was to be a Dream Car for middle-America, designed specifically for the flourishing US market. Designed by Spike Rhiando, an American, it was derived from the fashionable Austin A55. Spike wanted it built in fibreglass by a process of his own called rhiteglass with a huge front and rear overhang and tailfins that swooped skywards behind the perspex rear window. The convertible roof was aluminium, the bumpers were chromium plated steel tubes. The first Shamrock was built and photographed outside Feeney's shop, a natty young man behind the wheel. It looked startling against the dour wooden shopfront, glistening like a newly-landed flying saucer.

But Castleblayney's hour had not yet come. It would be another decade before 'Blayney would become the capital of American culture in Ireland, the Nashville of Europe, the hub of a Country and Western wagon-wheel extending to the outer rims of Ireland. The convulsion of the 1960s would have to be experienced before Tony Loughman could start a public house called El Ponderoso, as a base for the Top Rank Organisation stable of Country and Western stars.

Only eight Shamrocks were ever built. Castleblayney could not yet master the symbols of American success. The market changed, the Austin A55 fell out of favour against newer designs, for America was in a mood for rapid change, and it was easily bored with the old trappings of status. Castleblayney had still to learn that the money would be made not in packaging the American Dream for Americans, but in selling it to the Irish.

The half century from the 1920s to the 1970s saw the disintegration of peasant society which was characteristic of the west. The small farmer existed at subsistence level. He cultivated for domestic consumption, selling his small surplus and buying the few things needed that were not supplied by the farm itself. By and large his neighbours did the same. It had to be a highly integrated cultural and social entity in order to survive, with strong bonds of kinship and mutual aid among neighbours. There was no competition, the society was conservative and seemingly self-perpetuating, open to easy romanticism. Meaningful contact with the world beyond was restricted to exiled relatives. One comparative study of peasant societies placed the small farmers of the Irish west, in terms of the amount of their produce which they consumed themselves, on a par with many of the Indian tribes of South America. Because they bought and sold little, money was relatively unimportant.

The expansion of the Irish economy in the 1960s turned the west into a money economy. With money came new kinds of distinction, class distinctions, and with class came status. Television brought images of success, the symbols of conspicuous consumption. The economic transformation favoured the strong, the ones with families and near neighbours. The isolated unmarried small farmers saw most of their remaining ties with the old society swept away.

On the eve of Ireland's entry into the European Economic Community in 1973, there was in the west, instead of the earlier self-reliant class of small-scale subsistence farmers, a deprived and largely disillusioned remnant, unhappy with its present way of life and unsure of the future. This remnant was in no position to take advantage of the rapid flow of EEC funds into the Irish countryside. Instead of being lifted along with the rising tide, they were submerged in it, ever more isolated as modernisation increased in pace for the ones who could adapt.

With the passing of the peasant society went its culture. Those who survived took what suited them and adapted to the new times. They expressed their aspirations in their houses, their cars, their music, their clothes. But the old society did not die a sudden death. If it collapsed as an integrated entity, many of its parts remained, scattered, disparate, struggling side by side with the new icons.

The west today is like a spliced up newsreel, the shots out of sequence, the images superimposed on each other. One world is on its last legs; the other is rapidly running out of the bland self-confidence which fuelled its creation. But the process is irreversible. The plastic sachet of mud from the Reagan ancestral fields (which you can buy for thirty pence in the Ronald Reagan Bar, Ballyporeen) is as much a part of the soil of Ireland as is the cold clay that covers de Valera's bones.

A Fair Day, 1984.

89

KING OF THE HEARTLAND
Paschal Mooney's Kind of Country

"Applause applause applause," says the floor manager "and cue Paschal." Paschal Mooney hobbles out from the wings to join Philomena Begley in the centre of the Cork Opera House stage. "Howya Philomena. You're looking well. Is everything going okay? Now you just say yes." "Yes," says Philomena. The floor manager takes Paschal by the shoulders and half-turns him towards the right hand camera. "Now I'll just ask you the title of your next number, and you tell me." "It's called Country Girl," says Philomena.

Before the rehearsal of her numbers for RTE's "Country Star- time", Philomena Begley's band lounged around on the seats at the back of the hall. When their turn came she rounded them up. "Right come on, get up on that fuckin' stage." Noticing me behind her, she turned and smiled. "Oh dear, I shouldn't have said that, should I? It'll be all over the papers."

"Be yourself," says Paschal Mooney. "That's the one thing my mother always told me - Be yourself. When I started out trying to break into this business and doing auditions, I always tried to be someone else." Even when he was nine years old, Paschal used to make his own radio programmes on his father's tape recorder, taping the songs and putting in his own voice over the DJ's. When he was fifteen he made a complete audition tape and sent it to Radio Caroline. "It must have been terrible - real transatlantic stuff. I had no real voice of my own." He never heard anything more about it.

When he did find his own voice, it was to be the voice of small-town Ireland. "There are those," he says "who want to forget where they came from. People who leave rural Ireland, the last thing they want to be reminded of is Big Tom playing at the Saturday night dance. You see them down home at the weekend, and they're saying 'The dancehalls are terrible - full of cowboys and dirty old men trying to grope you.' Then they're back in Dublin, and they're down around the Leeson Street strip, off to Zhivago's and going home with married men. Young people have sadly discarded the old ways. Not everything that's old is bad."

Oh the streets of Dublin city
Can be friendly and so bright
But sometimes it can be lonely
Seeking strangers in the night.

Paschal, who was born in Drumshambo, County Leitrim, on 14 October, 1947, has the same birthday as Eamon de Valera and Cliff Richard. ("That's why I always preferred Cliff to Elvis as a youngster.") His father, Joseph Mooney, who is Chairman of Leitrim County Council and of the North Western Regional Tourism Organisation, was the local correspondent for a number of newspapers, and Paschal, having failed to become a radio star, set his heart on journalism. When he left school, he took a one-year course in journalism at Carrick-on-Shannon Vocational School. But there was no work on the local paper, so after a year as a merchandiser for the local jam factory, he left Leitrim for London. "I wanted the opportunity to move away from home, but I always saw myself coming back."

In London Paschal worked for employment agencies, became a member of the Institute of Employment Agency Consultants, and listened to The Beatles and The Rolling Stones like everybody else. When the first Wembley International Country Music Festival was held in 1969, he didn't bother going.

In 1970, however, the call to journalism finally came. He started writing about Irish bands in Britain for *Spotlight Magazine*, and the following year he got a regular music column in *The Irish Post*. "By 1971 I had actually started to like the stuff," he says "and I discovered that there was no real agency doing publicity and promotion for Irish country bands, so I started doing that as well." His new work brought him back and forth to Ireland, and in 1974 he moved back for good.

At a reception in the Montrose Hotel to mark the presentation of a silver disc to John Kerr for "Three-Leaved Shamrock", Paschal met Tony Gaynor who was producing "Country Music Time" on RTE radio. They talked about the need for an American country slot in the programme, and Gaynor said "If you can come up with the top five country records in the USA every week, you can present the slot yourself without an audition." So Paschal headed for the airport, found a stewardess on the New York flight and persuaded her to buy him the five records every week.

Noel Andrews was presenting "Irish Country Time", but Paschal gradually eased his way into more control of the programme, first doing a news slot and then taking on interviews as well. By 1977, he was doing interviews full time, scripting the programme and compiling all the records to be played. Ten days before Radio 2 opened in 1979, he was told that he would be presenting its new country music programme. He had already turned down an offer of a staff position as a sports reporter with the station. "I remember the last Saturday programme we did on Radio 1. Noel Andrews knew that he'd got nothing, and I knew that I'd got the new programme instead of him. All I could say to him was - Look I know nothing about all this - they've just told me."

Paschal thinks that too much of the content of Radio 2 programmes reflects the personal tastes of the presenters and producers. "This is a public broadcasting service," he says "and the important word is service. I'm into giving people what they want to hear. Irish people are attracted to country music because it's sentimental, and, above all, because it has a story they can identify with. People can readily identify with a song about a fella or a girl who has been blown out and is sitting in the bar getting stoned."

"The Lonely Hearts Club," he says "started as a pen-pal club of the air, but now it has developed into a boy-meets-girl situation. We've had three marriages that we know of so far." Some of the letters are country songs without the music. Jan, a forty-two year old divorcee from Scotland, who describes herself as a "honey blonde" and "a very lonely person", writes: "I couldn't go through a Christmas or New Year like I did last year." "I feel a great responsibility," says Paschal. "The response that someone gets depends on the way I convey the feeling and spirit of their letter."

John, from County Tyrone, is fifty, lives in a very nice bungalow and has his own phone. He is, like Paschal, a tee-totaller. He enjoys cooking. "Well, of course," says Paschal after reading out John's letter on the air, "when you're a bachelor you get into cooking very quickly. I have to look after myself too. You do get used to it, and it's not true to say that fellas aren't able to look after themselves or make a cup of tea for themselves. There may be some, but those of us that were kicked out of the mother's nest early on have got used to doing things for oneself. So ladies, girls - I'll call you girls, you like being called girls - it's a compliment - if you are into wanting to have a pen-pal relationship with somebody, and that sort of letter suits your purposes, well why not go ahead, because otherwise you'll be doing what Boxcar Willie is doing. You'll be having a bad case of feeling sorry for yourself, and that's really being very negative."

I want you so but I know it just can't be
I got a bad case of feelin' sorry for me.

Ronnie Griffiths sat at the back of the Cork Opera House watching Paschal Mooney rehearse his informal chat with the singers on stage. Ronnie has been singing professionally for twenty years, since he was fourteen. "There are two things that keep you going. One is seeing the success of somebody like Paschal, who sticks by what he believes in and can't be bought. The other is when Big Tom gets to number one. Big Tom is what it's all about. A fella goes to a dance and he sees Tom up there on stage and he thinks 'I could sing as well as him and I'm certainly no worse lookin' than he is.' So he doesn't see Big Tom as a threat, he identifies with him. And if you're a country singer and you see Big Tom get to number one, you think 'Well, maybe it could be me.' Big Tom gives us all hope."

Big Tom thinks that Paschal has done "great work for the music". "He has real feeling for country music," he says. "He understands what we are doing. Paschal knows all the pitfalls of the business and he deserves all the success he's had."

The rehearsals are over. The Opera House is filling up with people who have paid 3 each to take part in the recording of "Country Star Time", and Paschal Mooney is there to greet them. He rolls up the leg of his trousers to show the bulky white plaster. "Is there anybody here who doesn't know what happened to that leg?" Of course they all know about the accident about a mile from Drumshambo when a German driver ploughed into Paschal's car and smashed his leg. But the question automatically identifies them as a group, from the twelve-year old children to the famous Derry Gaelic footballer Micky Niblock, who has travelled down for the occasion. They belong together, and they belong with Paschal.

Paschal's patter is homely, a judicious mixture of plain religion and mild suggestiveness, perfectly pitched at getting the audience to do what it is told. He explains that Frank McCaffrey will not be appearing because of a road accident. "His car has joined mine I'm afraid, but sure it's God's will. Providence."

"Now," he exhorts "we want a real live feel to the show. So give good strong applause at the end of the songs and clap along if you feel like it. Don't worry about telling the priest in confession what you did - just do it. If you feel like taking your clothes off..." He smiles at the nun in the second row. "Oh sorry sister!" Then a more serious tone: "Now remember this programme will be billed as coming from the Cork Opera House, so you won't want to let your side down."

Diane if you're gonna do him wrong again
You might as well do the wrong again with me.

Brendan Quinn sings "Angeline", a song about a married man picking up a married woman in a bar, and "Sleeping Alone", in which the singer explains that he is "not putting down" one night stands, while six nuns in a row tap their feet and clap along. Then it's straight into "Momma's Angels".

A small band of angels came to visit Momma
And while they talked my Momma walked
Through Heaven's open door.

The audience dutifully plays its part. The musicians mime to pre-recorded backing tracks, and the singers perform for the cameras only. When the performance is halted for the third time by the technicians demanding a re-take, Paschal is there to keep everybody happy. "Sure you're enjoying it, aren't ye?" He fills in the gaps by explaining that all this technical stuff has really nothing to do with him. "The director Bil Keating thinks up all these things at night in bed. Other people do other things in bed. Well so does he - but he doesn't tell anybody about it." When the the re-take calls for a burst of applause, the audience responds with enthusiasm. Paschal holds up his hands to signal the applause, then drops them suddenly. The audience stops clapping.

Paschal feels that the great virtue of country music audiences is their tolerance. "They are less inclined to knock. Your average pop listener looks down on country, but that doesn't go the other way round". He says that the music brings people together, North and South, Catholic and Protestant.

To the land of my heart
Through the heart of my land
I am wandering tonight in my dreams

Paschal Mooney made his first political speech in 1969 when his father, Joseph, was a Fianna Fail candidate in the general election in Sligo-Leitrim. Joseph Mooney has been a member of Leitrim County Council since 1943 when he took over the seat

94

belonginging to his father, Andrew Mooney. His father who had been in Sinn Fein and then Cumann na nGaedheal, died just before the 1943 election, so Joseph had his election address printed on the other side of his father's and he was elected as an independent councillor. He joined Fianna Fail in 1960 and was made a Senator by Sean Lemass the following year.

Paschal was elected to the Fianna Fail National Executive (the "Big Fifteen") in 1978 and has held his position since. He hasn't stood for public office yet because he "can't afford to." "I've only been making a comfortable living for the past few years in show business. Going into politics at this stage would be a big financial risk. We don't pay our politicians enough, and as a result we get bad politicians. The glory aspect of politics means nothing to me, no more than Tom here (Big Tom is sitting beside him) would be worried about glory. As the fella said 'Fuck the glory and gimme the money.' Big Tom makes to say something, but Paschal grins: 'Don't mind Tom there, he's only an oul' Blueshirt.'"

Paschal Mooney intends to be a Government minister. "If I'm going to make a move, I'll have to make a move in the next few years. I'm more interested in getting involved on the international level rather than the local level. I couldn't see myself being a parish pump politican, a glorified messenger boy. Real power lies in being a minister."

He sees his best chance of gaining office as being through the next European Parliament elections. "The European election is a personality-style election, and people vote for candidates they wouldn't normally support. It's not really about policies at all." He has no strong policy views and doesn't particularly care who leads Fianna Fail. "I admire Charles Haughey because he has a very good brain, but it makes no difference to me - I would give the same loyalty to any leader because they are the leader."

Paschal Mooney's main political concern is "the national aspiration". "People want peace," he says. "Look at poor Big Tom coming home and not knowing what's going on, if someone is trying to kidnap him or what. Just give people a house, a job, and a car. Let the politicians rule."

Well the meek they inherited nothin'
The leaders are fallin' behind
So I'm singin' my song to the deaf men
Dancin' my dance to the blind.

The evening at the Opera House is drawing to a close. Paschal steps forward and takes the mike. "You've been a lovely audience. Good night and God bless you. But first will you please stand for the National Anthem." In one movement a whole crowd rises to its feet and stands rigidly to attention while Charlie Arkins of the Cotton Mill Boys plays a bluegrass version of the Soldier's Song on his electric fiddle.

In Dublin, December 1981.

IRELAND'S GONE WEST

On their first night home from Las Vegas, where they played the Stardust Lounge on the Strip of Broken Dreams (three shows a night and every one packed out) the Big 8 were mobbed. Two thousand people packed the dancehall, another thousand outside smashing the glass doors trying to get in. Brendan Bowyer, Tom Dunphy, Paddy Cole and Twink were pushed through the crowd by big country policemen eventually getting to the stage by a disused fire escape. The Big 8 were a slick, smooth showband; versatile, professional and sophisticated. But what mattered was that they had conquered America; had the queues leading half way down the Strip while Englebert Humperdinck was playing to half-empty houses in the same town. They were hailed as heroes and became the biggest draw in the dancehalls of Ireland. "Here we were all the way from Vegas, coming down to the arsehole of Mayo" says Twink. "They thought we had landed from Mars."

When they returned to Ireland three years later, in 1974, the Big 8 were trying to catch up. It no longer mattered that they went down big in America. America had been absorbed in the dancehalls of Ireland. Merged with the native product, Country and Western was becoming the staple dance music.

Twink, (her real name is Adele King) sang in the dancehalls for 10 years and already in Vegas she could sense what was happening. The band played half the year in Vegas, the other half in Ireland. To stay ahead of the pack in Ireland, they had to stay in touch with the mood at home.

"The Big 8 was very much a pop band, and we were very popular, but things were changing. One thing about the dancehalls is that crowds follow crowds. More than they follow a band, they follow a band that attracts a big crowd, because that way you're sure of meeting a girl or a fella. In Vegas Brendan Bowyer and the others started to notice that there were a lot of bands coming up that people had never heard of, that were beginning to attract crowds. They realised that it was what they were playing rather than the stars in the band that was pulling the crowds. We used to rehearse our coming-home programme about a month before we left Vegas and as the years crept by, from 1970 to 1974, our manager would always slip home and come back with a suitcase full of records for us to rehearse. And I noticed the influences were getting more and more Country and Western."

Twink had started at the age of 13, in the early 1960s, when the ballrooms of the West were in their heyday. The music then was pop, jive, big band jazz - a smooth transatlantic sound. America was always the source of the ballroom sound, copied directly from the movies and the records, with little local variation. "The nearer to Boston you get," she says, "the bigger the halls are. The real outposts like the Pontoon were huge. I remember the first time I played there thinking that it was like a hangar for an enormous aeroplane. I remember seeing the place when the Big 8 were really popular - it was absolutely jammed. You never saw the floorboards because they were dancing so close together and at that stage there must have been 2,500 to 3,000 people, which is really frightening."

Typically the ballrooms are owned and managed by a local man, a large farmer who also owns the grocery shop and the petrol pump, a man of substance who cares about money. "Those guys were up at six in the morning, out in the fields, giving the foxes lessons in cuteness. Money - lots of money, but the sort you wouldn't think had an arse in his trousers to look at him. They'd be always whinging and they always - to a man almost - always hated paying you. And it didn't matter how many you put in that ballroom. They always had the sob story, the whinge, afterwards. You could count on one hand the number who would come up and say 'There's your money as agreed.' There were times when you couldn't get an extra body in the hall short of having your granny hanging out of the chandelier. The owner would still come in and say 'It's a bit down, the crowd tonight. It wasn't as good as we thought it would be'."

One of these gentlemen I asked one time 'Where do I change?' And he looked at me like I had 40 heads and said 'What are you lookin' for?' And I said 'I'm looking for a room, preferably with a sink and a toilet in it.' And as he begrudgingly marched me down the hall to bring me to the priest's house to change he told me that us bloody city ones were all the same and if it was good enough for the Country and Western singers like Philomena Begley he didn't see why it shouldn't be good enough for me. I hated every living minute of it. I don't think I realised at the time how much I hated it, how much it was eating my soul away."

Micheal O hEithir never had a chance. The pub, admittedly, was in the heart of Cork and the county's hurlers were locked in epic battle with Limerick. But the radio went off with hardly a murmur of dissent as Dave, resplendent in white stetson, cowboy shirt and stencil tie, suede fringed waistcoat and knee-length leather boots made his way to the microphone. He strummed his guitar once then muttered a few words in a thick Cork accent. He opened his mouth to sing: "Well ah got a letter from a Buddy in Austin /I ain't seen for ten yeuhs or more /It started Dear Dave I'm glad that you've made it /'Cause you were so God blessed poor..." Dave has never been to America but he wants to go someday, to Nashville, Tennessee. He dreams of being a country star. He dreams of making it big. After all, every one of the great country singers started poor and made it to the top.

Don Gibson is a living legend. Born in the foot-hills of North Carolina, poor white trash, he is now one of three men in the world who have written a song that has sold four million copies. "I Can't Stop Lovin' You" is a country standard, as is "Oh Lonesome Me", which he also wrote, and he has 200 other country songs to his credit, including "Sweet Dreams" and "One Day at a Time". "I was brought up poor but I'm not poor anymore," he says.

Don Gibson doesn't believe the country and western dream anymore. At the Carling International Country Music Festival in Cork last week he sang four songs, repeated two of them and disappeared. He recently recorded an album of his greatest hits for K-Tel Records in America. "I went into the studio and there were all these musicians there that I'd never seen before in my life. I didn't say nothin' to them. I just put the earphones on and I recorded sixteen tracks in three and a half hours. It didn't mean nothin', it was just mechanical. After twenty years in country music it just didn't matter anymore; I came out and I said to my manager 'This is no good. It's just mechanical.' He said to me 'This is just fine. It's just what they want.'"

"So then they gave me a big cheque and I took it. When I started out there was good times. Now it's all changed. I'm not into it anymore, but sometimes it makes me sad." Don Gibson is rich but he doesn't write songs anymore. "I guess the spark's not there now," he says.

Tony Loughman also says he has "thrown in the towel". He is the kingpin of Irish country music and his Top Rank Organisation made Castleblayney, County Monaghan, into Ireland's Nashville. In the seventies he controlled the scene from his base in the Three Star Inn, named after his three biggest acts: Big Tom, Philomena Begley and Susan McCann. He still manages Susan McCann and Roly Daniels, but he believes that the halcyon days are over.

Like the stars he has managed, he came up the hard way and rode the great country and western boom for all it was worth. Now the boom is over and he is, he says, "taking it easy".For years he worked in a quarry outside Castleblayney, and 20 years ago, when a bit of prosperity began to worm its way into the countryside, he started to run dances in marquees during the summer. "I had a few good years after that," he says, "but now there's far safer investments than country music."

When Tony Loughman was working in a quarry, Susan McCann was growing up "on bacon and cabbage and hard work" on a small farm in South Armagh. "We were very rural and very poor," she remembers. Their farm was too small to support them by itself and her father worked "like a slave" in the fields of the bigger, more prosperous farmers around him, stooping in the fields. She remembers getting on her bike to bring him his lunch to the neighbour's farm where he was working. "They were so mean and they cared so little about a low farm labourer that they wouldn't even give him his dinner in the house."

There was always music in the McCann house. Her father played traditional music on the accordion and when Susan sang as a girl the songs were generally traditional ones. When she relaxes with friends now, they often go to the local Comhaltas Ceoltoiri Eireann gatherings and occasionally she will sing a folk song for them. Her husband, Denis Heaney, whom she met through singing in local semi-professional bands, also played the accordion and was Comhaltas Ulster champion accordion player at the age of 14. These days he plays electronic keyboards in The Storytellers, his wife's backing group. "Times changed and he had to change with them," says Susan. The old days of poverty are gone now, she says. "Thank God it has all changed. There is no upper or middle-class anymore. Everyone is reasonably well off. I still mix with the people I was reared with. I haven't changed."

The changing times brought a new music. From the early 1960s the big showbands like The Capitol began to include a few country numbers in their set. In 1964 Jim Reeves came to tour Ireland and popularised the country sound as no one had before. There were immediate echoes for the music in Ireland. Country had its roots in the Irish music brought to the Southern states by the hard men who built the railroads. (When Susan McCann played in Texas last year

100

her backing band started a traditional session in the dressing rooms backstage which ended with 45 American country musicians joining in.)

And the simple stories which the country songs told were greatly to the Irish taste ("The songs are about basic things like people dyin' and people gettin' jilted," says Paddy Cole, who has played the ballrooms and cabaret rooms of Ireland for almost a quarter of a century, "and we have plenty of both in Ireland." "Irish people love tears and blood," says Susan McCann, "and that's what they get in country songs.")

But such echoes do not create an industry. For the ballroom owners and the promoters of the circuit, country was a godsend.

It is the ballroom owners who decide the musical taste of the country people. "It's a game of very careful planning in the band programme," says Twink. "Most of the big bands know this instinctively, what to play in certain areas. Most of the smaller bands had some kind of pride and they wanted to play what they wanted to play . The owners would come up to them and say 'That kind of rubbish doesn't go down here at all now. You'll not get another booking here playing that kind of crap. Play something that the people want to hear.' They would come up to you in the middle of the night, in a break between sets and say 'You have to change your programme.' The ballroom owner decided what the punters wanted to hear in their area. They had it all worked out to a fine art."

And all over the west the art was Country'n'Western. Until the mid-1960s the punters had accepted mainstream commercial music, the same smooth rhythms that had them swaying in Dublin and London and downtown Boston. It was an American sound. But as the focus of popular music shifted from America to the hard fast urban sound of the Mersey Beat, a slow rebellion began to shape itself; a rebellion against this new commercial mainstream.

"What got their backs up was when the pop music started to take a very English influence, with it coming across from nearer shores. 'The beat's changed', they'd tell you. And they didn't like this change of beat. I think they looked for an option. I think it was looking back to further shores."

Hank Williams and Hank Snow, Tom T Hall and Jim Reeves were played on the radio and now a group called The Smokey Mountain Ramblers started to play bluegrass country music round the halls. "They were huge. Suddenly people found something they could stomp their feet to again. And then gradually the interest broadened and suddenly you noticed that the record sales were very American-

101

biased rather than British."

"And of course the demise of the old showbands like the Dixies and the Capitol, saw the upsurge of a new type band, which was now beginning to adopt the American suits. The mohair ones of the showband era were turning more into the cowboy look with the stencil tie and the cuban-heel boots. It was clutching on to a more honest-to-God beat, something you could get a grip on and stamp your boots to. It was like a defiance of British pop."

Paddy Cole played with the elite of the showbands, The Capitol, and he remembers ballroom managers complaining to him that The Capitol were setting too high a standard. The slick, sophisticated, highly polished sounds of the best showbands were difficult to emulate. Bands of that quality were in short supply and were therefore in a position to make strong demands on the ballroom owners.

But country music was simple and almost anyone could play it. All you needed was a rhythm section and a singer, instead of the showband frontline of trumpet, trombone and sax. "Country became a fad overnight," says Paddy Cole. "There were hundreds of bands joining in the boom. It was a better music for the ballroom owners because more people could play it." By the mid-sixties there were almost 700 professional bands making a living out of the ballroom circuit in Ireland. (Now there are about 100).

And it wasn't just the ballroom owners who benefited. "It was a hell of an industry in the 1960s," says Paddy Cole. "When there was a dance in Castleblayney practically the whole town was making money out of it: the hotels, the pubs, the hairdressers, the garages, the boutiques - we called them clothes shops then - they were all turning over a tidy few shillings. It was a big part of the economy."

In the early sixties ballrooms went up almost overnight, many of them little more than four walls slapped up in a field. Some families, such as the Reynolds brothers Albert and Jim, ran whole chains of ballrooms. "They were four walls and a stage and a thing the size of a telephone box which was called a dressing room for the band," remembers Paddy Cole. "There was a lot of infighting between the chains and a lot of efforts to monopolise the circuit. Bands were told 'You play for the right price or you don't get any dates in maybe a dozen venues.'"

Suddenly the bands needed protection. "Most of the showbands had someone in the band who would do their bookings for them," says Paddy Cole, "but when the boom came the professional managers came into their own." Petty corruption was endemic. "The bands had to pay someone to watch at the door and check on the number of people going in, because they were paid on a percentage of the takings. There was a famous story of T.J. Byrne when he was manager of the Big 8 taking a stroll out from the ballroom when a dance was beginning and finding the ballroom owner out on the road half a mile away from the hall with a bus conductor's bag over his shoulder selling tickets for the dance."

To break it big a band needed the protection of a manager like Tony Loughman. For a younger singer or a young band it was important to become part of a stable of acts which had big names among its ranks. A wily manager could use his bigger attractions as leverage to get dates for the small bands. There were no threats, just gentle hints. "If you're onto a hotel owner or a dancehall owner," says Tony Loughman, "you're selling a small act, the owner might tend to say to himself 'I'll give Loughman the booking because he has Susan McCann as well and it's no harm to keep on his good side. There's no point in giving the date to a fella that only manages a small band.' You're being screwed in a nice way.

"But the promoters are worse than the managers. I remember one promoter in Wexford and whenever you'd ring him about money he'd put on his mother's voice and pretend he wasn't there. The ballroom owners were mostly farmers or shopkeepers and a lot of them made big money and got out fast. Even big bands were often very badly paid. It was a screw job. Promoters screwed the bands. And it's still the same. If you have what they want you screw them, if you haven't they screw you. And if you're stuck you might have to take it because you have to pay the wages at the end of the week."

But it wasn't only the bands and the promoters who were getting screwed. Behind all the deals and all the music was the real business of the ballrooms: the promise of sex.

"I know girls used to tell me," says Twink, "that you could be lambasted from the pulpit if you were seen carrying on disgracefully after a dance. Those country parish priests would read you the hell-and-high-water book. And therefore the girls tried to keep the image as 'Oh sure I wouldn't do that at all, Michael. You're a terrible man.' But it was very pretentious. The devilment that went on in the streets afterwards was nothing ordinary. There's always a chip wagon outside the dancehall and that was a great meeting place. After the dance, if you'd half scored at all, it would be 'I'll meet you down by the chip wagon.' Our van would inevitably be parked somewhere round the chip wagon, because it was inevitably in the most convenient place, and you could watch what was going on. God, I was astonished! They were so outrageous in their conduct. It must have been like the fox and the grapes: the harder it was to get, the sweeter a bit of juice was.

"The one thing that astonished me was the amount of groupies that there were around the country. Nice respectable country girls, and they hung round our boys in the band. There was no shortage of takers after the dance for the wagon or the dressingroom, or the back of the ballroom. I remember waiting around on my own in the car park on cold freezing nights, until eventually I'd have to go to the van and demand that they get out."

Into this world came Susan McCann. She sang at dances and carnivals within a fifty mile radius of her home, in Down, Armagh, Monaghan and Louth, a couple of nights a week from the time she was 16. One of the promoters she played for was Tony Loughman. After a few years she and Denis decided to settle down and give up the dancehall business. She took up hairdressing, he did accountancy. In 1977 she met Tony Loughman again at a show and he persuaded her to go back to the business. She laid down the condition that she would not work more than 60-miles from her home in Newry. She hoped, she says, "to help with the mortgage." She is now probably the most successful European country singer and plays regularly in a number of continental countries, particularly Norway and Switzerland. "There's one reason why I made it," she says. "I had good management."

Tony Loughman is very clear about the kind of music he likes. "Country is popular with rural people because it's laid back and not noisy. I don't like 'progressive' country and I can't stand this heavy stuff. I like commercial pop and most of all I like middle-of-the-road country." Susan McCann doesn't talk much about her own tastes. It's what the punters want that matters. "I read my audience fairly quickly by the applause that I'm getting and I'll change the music to suit. Most audiences like to have their hankies wet now and then. The older audience loves the 'poor mammy' type of songs. I sing to suit the crowd, not myself. I have to please everybody, not just a small few." At the Carling festival she sang "The Banks Of My Own Lovely Lee" twice for a delighted Cork audience, reading the words from a sheet of paper.

On stage she manages to be perfectly ambiguous, combining glamour with homeliness, a whiff of illicit sex with a cosy reaffirmation of traditional values. She looks good in ballgowns or satin trousers, but never unapproachable. She sings of adultery and infidelity ("There's as much of that going on over here as there is in America, even though it's not supposed to, so people can still relate to those songs") and sex ('*So if I die and go to Heaven/It won't be nothing new/'Cos I think that I saw Heaven/While I was making love to you*'). But in the middle of a song about a married woman running away from home with another man she goes over to her husband Denis at the keyboard and puts her arms around him. The audience loves it.

Although she is now one of the biggest names in the Irish entertainment industry, Susan McCann is careful to keep as close as possible to her audiences. Country music is a great leveller - its lack of sophistication keeps the performer close to the audience. "Even if some of the country singers can't sing very well," says one promoter, "that's no great harm - it gives the ordinary fella looking on the feeling that he's not too far from stardom himself." Susan McCann always tries to be available for autographs after a show. When she plays in Northern Ireland she is careful never to distance herself from the allegiances of her audience. "If I have to play 'The Soldier's Song' at the end of the night, I'll play 'The Soldier's Song'. If I have to play 'The Queen', I'll play 'The Queen.'" She is not a social climber. "I won't tolerate snobbery. You get people at home who didn't want to know you when you were a housewife, but they want to know you now that you're a big name. I feel very strongly about that and I just won't stand for it."

In the last two years Susan McCann's repertoire for her shows in Ireland has become less and less based on country and western music. Country is the music of the dancehalls and the dancehalls have been going through a recession. At the Carling Festival in Cork Susan McCann's performance was as much cabaret as country. Even The Cotton Mill Boys, always the most diehard purists among the country bands, have added a touch of sex to their line-up in the person of skimply clad Sharon King. The country music industry is on the defensive. Tony Loughman has thrown in the towel.

"Ten years ago," he says, "all the bands were doing good business. Then there was only dancing or football for diversion and people used to go dancing four or five nights a week, without any exaggeration. Now there's counter-attractions - there's badminton, golf, swimming, jogging, even in a town like Castleblayney. Also people are more advanced - a fella can take a girl back to his house

105

now whereas a few years ago he couldn't do that unless they were engaged. Even though people have more leisure time now the ballrooms that closed are not really missed."

He blames the pernicious influence of the city, exercised through the medium of RTE Radio 2. "City people knock the music. DJs and producers in RTE don't know what's happening in Castleblayney or Tralee or Ballyhaunis. You tell them that Big Tom got 1,500 people in Tralee on a Wednesday night and they say: 'So what?.'

"I pity them really. These people in RTE don't know what they are. They think outside Dublin there's nothing else. They're afraid their friends might laugh at them if they played a country record. There's a lot of pseudos involved up there. If you go into RTE 2 they just laugh at you. A lot of them RTE DJs are just failed showband singers themselves and it's all sour grapes. As soon as I get to the steps of RTE, I get depressed. I remember going in there with the Nashville album that Porter Wagoner produced for Susan McCann and giving it to a producer in Radio 2. He just caught it by one end and flung it in the corner. 'Don't bring me in shit like that, Tony' he said. With that kind of attitude, I accept defeat and that's not my form."

Susan McCann is the last of the big Irish country stars. She emerged into the big time nearly eight years ago and since then not a single new country singer or band has made it. There is no longer fast money to be made as there was in the days of the ballroom boom and the businessmen who own the industry are loath to take risks. Tony Loughman says that he is still seeing bands with every bit as much talent as those that made it in the sixties, but the money is not available to sell them on the market. "A week wouldn't go by but some mammy or daddy is asking me to listen to a band or a singer and to please people I might go to hear four or five. Some of them are very good but I have to say there's nothing I can do. They don't realise that I'd have to spend £50,000 to make a band and there's far safer things to do with that kind of money. You can spend £15,000 on an album and get five airplays. You have to promote a band in the same way you promote Persil or lager and if you can't do that you don't get the airplay. There's no future for young bands. I've given up."

From next September Susan McCann, the last Queen of Irish Country will begin to cut back on her dates and play more in Europe and America. The country boom is on the wane, though it has left an abiding impression. There is still a big country following

106

and there is still money to be made on a smaller scale. As Tony Loughman says: "For every dancehall that closes, a loungebar gets bigger."

"A Fair Day", 1984/The Sunday Tribune, June, 1984.

BRIGHT WITH COSY HOMESTEADS

"For the first four years of my life I lived in a two-roomed thatched cottage rented by my father at two shillings per week. The floor area was about 300 square feet. The furniture consisted of a settle bed full of rubbish and rats, a table, iron bed and a few chairs. It had a front door and two tiny windows. Built in a hole on the side of a hill, if you can imagine such a situation, it blended into the landscape, surrounded by privet-hedges, whitethorn bushes and trees. I have still nostalgic memories of the cricket in the hearth and the high, thatched, smoke blackened ceiling. But animals now would not be housed in such conditions."

The words are those of Jack Fitzsimons, author of a book, *Bungalow Bliss*, which has gone into seven editions since 1971, a book that has helped to change the face of the Irish countryside. In the last decade, the despised thatched cabins of Jack Fitzsimons' boyhood, picturesque, at ease with the soft Irish landscape, have been swept away in a fervour of house building. No more rat-infested settlebeds; no more tiny windows; no more blending into the landscape. The bliss of the new bungalow is its ostentation. For all the admonitions of architects and planners, it sits on the landscape like a beached whale, puffing and blowing to assert its presence. The modern Irish country house displays its assorted ornamentations, gathered from a bewildering variety of sources, as if they were peacock's feathers. It is not just a place to live - it is a direct expression of the dreams and aspirations of its owners, who are, usually also the designers.

The abandoned cottages that littered the Irish countryside were the most heart-rending reminder of the pain of mass emigration. But with the new rural prosperity, which came with Ireland's entry to the EEC in 1972, the building boom gathered momentum. By 1976, 5,500 new private bungalows were being built every year in the countryside. By 1981 that figure had doubled to 11,517. In 1982 and 1983 country bungalows were the biggest category of new housing, surpassing even the sprawling urban estates and accounting for 40% of the houses built in Ireland. Only 11% of the new country houses were designed by an architect.

When the money came in, the ground was levelled. Young couples talked into the night of the lovely arches they had seen in a magazine, of the picture window that was on the television. They went on reconnaisance missions around the countryside, spotting a nice coloured brick here, a sunburst doorway there, a wrought iron porch on the doctor's house and a plaster dog on the ballroom owner's gatepost.

"A young fella building a house now," says Pat O'Grady, one of the biggest builders in the Galway area, "he wants to do it his own way. Fellas go around with cameras and take photos of houses they like around the place and they'll ask you to put in this or that feature. You even get people bringing back photos from their holidays on the continent and maybe it's something they've seen in a magazine or on the television. Very few have money up front so they build the houses in stages as the money comes in and they get ideas as they go along."

At Knocknacarragh, on the road to Barna, is a house that Pat O'Grady built. Michael Paul, a very successful hairdresser, returned from America in the mid-seventies with the plans for his dream home in his pocket. It stands now at the gateway to Connemara, a huge monument to success in modern Ireland. It has all the features of the native version of the American dream home: white mock-adobe walls, a huge sun verandah beneath the grey Galway sky, a sweeping Spanish arch, wrought iron and coloured stone.

It is, says Pat O'Grady, the most popular house he has ever built. It is the symbol that people aspire to, looking to it for inspiration.

Bungalow Bliss is the great leveller of Irish rural society, a bible of social mobility. For £100 a young couple can buy a basic house plan and a schedule of building materials. With a free site from one of their parents and tax-free local labour, they can build a bungalow thousands of pounds cheaper than they could buy one on the open market. And they are free to take whatever images of success they most desire and use them in their own house.

The new bungalows are the perfect compromise between consumerist individualism and the desire to stay put in your own place, between the new values and the old.. They string themselves along the roads, instead of clustering into villages. "A young fella will gravitate towards his own townland where he grew up," says Pat O'Grady, "and often would be willing to travel 25 miles to work. He has his contacts at home and doesn't want to be institutionalised." The choice of sites has much more to do with the desire to stay close to where you were born than with the aesthetic considerations that concern planners and architects.

Traditionally, when houses were built in the Irish countryside, they were assembled from the few materials available locally: slate or thatched roofs and whitewashed walls or walls of stone or brick left to weather naturally. The uniformity of the houses reflected the poverty and relative social uniformity of the society. Nobody had much more than anyone else, so there was no need to compete. Because it reflected its society so well in its simplicity and humility, the traditional thatched cottage became more than just a house: it became the home of a myth, a symbol of pure Irishness. The athletic youths and comely maidens of de Valera's dream lived in a countryside "bright with cosy homesteads".

But having become a symbol of stability for one generation, the old cottage was a natural symbol of stagnation and decay for the next. It summed up all that was abhorrent to a new generation infinitely more conscious of class and status: it was low, mean, dingy, poky, above all uniform and classless. The new houses of the 1970s, on the other hand, are bright, open, ostentatious, and fiercely competitive. When people build their own houses, they are expressing their own sense of themselves. And what the great hacienda baroque villas of modern Ireland express is a mixture of confidence and insecurity: confidence in the ostentation, without thought to the surrounding landscape; insecurity in the obvious delight in going one better than the neighbours, the obvious terror of being left behind.

The belief that our houses in some way reflect our own moral worth is a deeply rooted one. In the foreword to *Bungalow Bliss*, Jack Fitzsimons wrote: "I always believed when growing up that people who live in big houses and look out through big windows must have a superior outlook, a desirable dimension to their character, that is denied to those who are brought up in poky rooms with puny windows - that they must have a deeper perception and broader outlook. The concept remains with me but the reality is not now so convincing."

The dream that simple architectural features can somehow increase the status of the homeowner has had a real effect on new Irish houses. Windows in Irish houses in recent years have gone from being traditionally vertical to being predominantly horizontal. Horizontal picture windows look brighter from the outside but in the Irish climate they in fact let in a good deal less light and are much less effective for ventilation. Yet they have become standard.

The dream has overtaken the reality.

Because they are the products of dreams and aspirations as much as practical realities, the bungalows often stand in stark opposition to their surroundings. Picture windows that might have looked happily out on the Californian sunshine are filled with the dull reflection of the bogs of Ireland. Spanish arches look like raised eyebrows, astonished to find themselves in the wetlands of Leitrim. A riot of different stones and bricks bursts forth, clashing wildly with each other and with the colours around. Multicoloured split concrete joins white adobe and red roof tiles and coloured plaster and dark wood - sometimes all on the same house. In the imitation stone facings, the regularity of the "irregularities" in the cast stone moulds shows that something is not quite as it should be.

What do the new bungalows aspire to? Self-expression, the proud independence of the hacienda-owner, Manolito in "The High Chaparral" shooting bandits and indians from the dazzling white patio.The greatest store of imagery for the new country houses is the Wild West. Many of the biggest new houses in places like Leitrim, Roscommon and Mayo belong to cattle dealers, the new aristocracy of the west, and the mythology of the big ranchers is strong. The cattle dealers build houses like "The High Chaparral" in County Mayo, with white picket fences and Mexican verandas and wagon-train cartwheels decorating the walls, and a horned bull's skull over the driveway entrance, houses that can only have been conceived in the midst of a cowboy fantasy. The sturdy independence and sentimental loyalties of the cowboy are the myths most easily associated with cattle and in a country where cattle are the biggest business there is, the appeal of those myths is enormous.

Nor is it surprising that the new bungalows, the most direct expression of the economic boom of the seventies in the Irish countryside, should look to America for the images that they employ. For over a century America had a deep link to rural Ireland through emigration, until the images of financial success began to be seen through American eyes.

The American cousins who had made it in the States sent back pictures and reports of the good life. Rural Ireland got used to looking to America for status symbols. Since the end of the Sixties, the decade dominated in Ireland by the influx of American money and industry, Country and Western has become the staple music of rural Ireland. The new bungalows are the embodiment of the spirit of Irish Country and Western, transplanting an American style to Irish soil. Like the music, the bungalows are democratic - almost

111

anyone can sing country and western; almost anyone can build a bungalow with *Bungalow Bliss*.

While the rest of the building trade is in recession, the bungalow boom continues unabated, the trail of bliss winding its way inexorably further out the road from almost every village in Ireland. The exhortations of experts have been utterly ineffective. For the urge to build and to build where people can see you, touches a deeper nerve in rural Ireland than ideals like respect for the landscape. For all that they are unattractive and sometimes absurd, the bungalows are an expression of faith in the future by a generation only a few years away from mass emigration. Their irony is that they are at the same time a product of a discontinuity, and of a faith in continuity, of the possibility of a future. That future may be founded on new insecurities taking the place of the old ones but the intention is clearly to stay put. The new generation in the countryside would rather own an American homestead in Ireland than pine for an Irish homestead in America.

"A Fair Day", 1984/The Sunday Tribune, April, 1984.

THE MAN OF YOUR DREAMS

"Pock". The Ball rebounds off the springy, flat wood of the bat and spins through the air towards an open hand waiting to grasp it. The ball is bowled again. "Pock". It is the sound of high blue skies, airless days and lush, rich greenery but it echoes now off dull unplastered concrete as the ball traces its way through the grey overbearing skies of a Mayo Sunday. The cricketers' brown skin and black, shiny hair stand out all the more against the fierce whiteness of their open-necked shirts, their dark arms sticking out below sleeves that are tightly rolled to just above the elbow. Little boys and their fathers playing together to pass the afternoon, they have no proper stumps, never mind a rolled, even crickety pitch. They toss the ball back and forth over the scrub ground littered with patches of gravel, broken concrete blocks, odd bits of building materials.

Behind them are their own houses, surrounded by a rough wall, facing away from the road as if turning their backs to the small town of Ballyhaunis in which they find themselves. In front of them, up a long tarmacadamed driveway, is a huge hulking new house, its roof as black as their hair, its walls as white as their shirts. The house, which the locals say cost a million pounds to build, could be a hugely inflated version of a normal country house, set as it is next to a stark, open quarry in landscape that looks mean and dishevelled - except that built into its facade are flowing Islamic arches, fantastic and arabesque. They give the house the lightness of a spaceship that has just landed on this alien terrain - that might, at any moment, take off into the overhanging clouds. It is the house of Sher Rafique, the Pakistani businessman who owns much of Ballyhaunis, and whose Halal meat plant employs the greater part of the male workforce.

A few yards down the road, inside the Midas Bar, Restaurant and Nite Club, the drains have to be unblocked, the ashtrays emptied, the broken glasses swept up. The stale smell of last night's dance still has to be exorcised and the rehearsals for tonight's talent contest are already behind schedule. While the cricketers swing luxuriantly, the owner of the Midas Club, Paul Claffey, is a whirl of activity, dragging tables, shunting chairs, doling out orders. "Get another barrel up...check the level on those mikes ..." In just a few hours, this old dance hall, littered with the lonesome evidence of last night's dissipations, will have to be transformed into a dream factory. Tonight 'Sunday Night Live at the Midas' features both the finals of the Zanussi Entertainer of the Year competition and another installment of Paul Claffey's own version of the television game show, 'The Price Is Right'. Tomorrow morning at the factory it may be all sheep's intestines and barrels of blood, but tonight at the dream factory it has to be sheep's eyes and barrels of beer. Already, on stage, a young woman with an enormous Irish harp is practising 'The Mountains of Mourne' and there's gangs of Paddies digging for gold in the streets.

Paul Claffey is thirty-four and has been in the entertainment business for nearly a quarter of a century. When he was ten he started running discos in the Marist Brothers school in Castlerea, a few miles across the Roscommon border from Ballyhaunis. During the summer holidays, he and three friends hired sound equipment and ran the disco in the school hall. For their pains, they made twelve shillings each. The other three reckoned that the returns were out of all proportion to the effort and gave up. Paul reckoned that four twelves would be forty-eight and two quid wasn't to be sneezed at, so he carried on on his own.

Shortly afterwards he noticed that there was always a row about whose turn it was to go up the town for Coke and crisps when the lads went to the swimming pool. He took his bike to the local Coke distributor, persuaded him to give him a crate on tick and started his own shop outside the swimming pool. By the time he was twelve, he was hiring function rooms in all the local towns, employing a driver to take himself and the disco gear around. He started booking live acts, bringing them down from Dublin to the dancehalls of the area. He was still so young that he had to pretend to the bands that the Paul Claffey who had booked them was unfortunately indisposed and that he had just been sent along with a message. By the mid-Seventies he had the leases on five of the biggest dancehalls in South Mayo, North Galway and Roscommon.

What made him was demographics. With a baby boom and very little emigration, there were plenty of young kids around, kids who identified with youth culture and not with country and western or middle-of-the-road cabaret. Paul Claffey spotted the gap in the

114

market and dived in, bringing rock acts like Brush Shields, The Freshmen and even Thin Lizzy to Ballyhaunis and Gort. Almost overnight, Horslips tapped a whole new market for indigenous rock music. Paul Claffey had them booked for £125 to play the Royal Cinema in Roscommon town. In between the booking and the gig, the band broke it big. He made his £125 back on the raffle at the interval.

But the tide of youth began to ebb as the Seventies gave way to the Eighties. There were fewer young people around as emigration began to edge upwards again. The High Court loosened restrictions on hotels getting bar extensions for cabarets and the dancehall boom was over. In four months, Paul Claffey lost all of his dancehalls and a pub. He was dragged through the courts over matters of money. He had just enough left to risk it all on getting a drinks license for the old dancehall in Ballyhaunis, now re-named The Midas Club. It cost him £65,000 but he did it. When he opened his doors and the young people who had been his regular customers arrived, they were discretely turned away. He had decided to go for the family market, the married couples and the middle-aged who had nothing to do on a Sunday night. Round here, there was no future in the young.

Bismillah allahu akbar! The slaughterman is looking down into the upturned face of the sheep. Only the sheep's neck and head stick out from the pen which holds it fast. The sheep enters, the pen closes and revolves, leaving its neck pointing upwards, ready for the blade of the slaughterman. The Koran lays down that an animal must be killed in the name of God and that it must be killed with a sharp knife, without violent blows. The prophet discouraged the eating of too much meat - "Don't," says the Koran, "make your stomachs the graveyard of animals" - and those animals which were killed were generally raised by the family and slaughtered with great respect and gravity by the head of the household. Muslims, however, have been eating more and more meat in recent years and the Prophet's injunctions have had to be adapted to industrialised production. In Ballyhaunis, a dozen Muslim slaughtermen - Egyptians, Turks, Syrians, Pakistanis - act as mullahs, muttering the prayer *Bismillah allahu akbar* (In the name of God, God is greater) while they sever with one cut the twin arteries of the throat, cutting off the supply of blood to the brain, causing loss of consciousness and death.

Twelve years ago, when Paul Claffey's dancehall empire was burgeoning, Sher Rafique built a small slaughtering shed by the side

115

of the road, on a one-acre site a few hundred yards outside Ballyhaunis. Now there are ten individual plants on the site and Halal (the name is the Islamic equivalent of kosher) is the biggest exporter of lamb from the country, the second biggest of beef. Sixty per cent of those exports go to the EEC, largely to the big ethnic Islamic market, the rest to North Africa and the Middle East. The plant now straggles half a mile out the road, one virtually unbroken blind wall of concrete. The far side of the road is littered with thousands of pounds worth of building materials: blocks, pipes, shores, posts, all strung out in a line going nowhere. Behind them is Sher Rafique's house and, the frame of its half-built dome naked against the sky, a mosque.

Those who frequent the mosque are never to be seen in the other gathering places of Ballyhaunis. They don't drink, so they don't go into the pubs. They don't dance, so they don't go into the `Midas. Aside from the children who attend the local national school, the Muslims are a familiar but largely enigmatic presence. When they eat in the restaurants, they generally want to be served quickly and be away again. Across the road from the entrance of the Midas, a family of Syrians lives, but Paul Claffey doesn't know much about them, except that they are decent, quiet people. It's not that anyone has a bad word to say about the people who increasingly provide the town's reason to exist,or that there is any obvious racism, just that everyone is happy enough for their presence to remain insulated and discreet. Once, one of the Muslim workers wandered into the Midas and asked for some 'white music'. He was given a tape of some Irish country and western and he left,never to return. When their presence does impinge, however, it does so very obliquely. At the Midas talent contest that Sunday evening, it is kept safely at a distance.

Suddenly, from the bank of speakers on the Midas stage, the 'Also sprach Zarathustra' music from '2001' blares out: *daah, daah,* da-da. "And now, ladies and gentlemen, " announces Paul Claffey, "with the time at twenty past the hour of ten o'clock, we present the Zanussi Entertainer of the Year final. And here is your host, the one and only John Duggan." John Duggan has already been on stage an hour before, to introduce Louise Morrissey and her band. Louise has changed out of her jeans and into a silver lame knee-length suit, the boys in the band have doffed their jumpers and put on their blue cowboy-style suits with knee-length jackets, white shirts, blue dicky-bows and shoes so black and shiny they make pure whiteness look dull. The two young girls who are always the first to take the floor in any dancehall have already danced on their own to 'My Tears Have Washed I Love You From The Blackboard Of My Heart', turning little twirls and pirouettes before being joined by a quickening trickle of dancers for 'The Night Daniel O'Donnell Came To Town' and 'The Green Glens Of Antrim'. The band have already finished their first set and John Duggan has been warning the crowd not to sit in the passageways. "You'll say to yourself 'Wasn't I an awful fool to sit here'." But the one and only John Duggan has to be introduced again, because now the show is being broadcast live on Paul Claffey's own pirate radio station, Mid-West Radio, the signal being beamed to much of Mayo, Galway, Sligo, Leitrim and Roscommon, from a tiny room at the back of the Midas.

John Duggan does the late evening easy-listening show on Mid-West Radio. He started doing it shortly after the station was established in November 1985. At the time, he had not yet retired from his job and was still serving as a garda in Glenamaddy. He had been in the guards long enough to remember serving in Crumlin garda station when it was one half of a thatched cottage shared with Saint Agnes GAA club. At night in Crumlin while he was watching over the cells, he would write little songs for T.R. Dallas and Hugo Duncan and, above all, for Brendan Shine, who had a big hit with one of them,'The Rose Of Castlerea'. He started doing his Mid-West Radio show as John Edwards, but someone made a complaint to the Garda authorities that it was improper for a member of the force to be working for an illegal station. There was an investigation, a file was sent down from Dublin, but then someone in charge said that they liked listening to his show and no action was taken.

John introduces the contestants one by one and has a few words with each before their set. Jackie, a local teacher, sings and plays the Celtic harp and wants to say hello over the radio to Father Stephen and all the First Years in the convent. Pauline from Ballagh sings Chris de Burgh and says that a Nancy Griffith song "reminds me of Ireland and the troubles we have here - if we work together maybe we can solve them". Dave from Kilbeggan has a matching hankie and tie and sings songs made famous by Joe Dolan, "a man who I've admired and loved for years". John reads out a request for a girl "who celebrates her birthday tomorrow and is off to America in the morning".

And then there is this black guy on stage, a black Irishman called

Luke Davis who comes from Westport and wears a really cool suit with rolled up sleeves and no tie. His voice is extraordinary, a cross between Desmond Dekker and Rod Stewart. He purrs and shouts and growls. He sings his own composition with just an acoustic guitar accompaniment. He poses and prowls. He's as Irish as anyone, but here in the Midas there is something foreign and exotic about him. Something that must be kept at a distance. When the judges, local teachers and journalists and businessmen, come to vote for the prizewinners, no one places him first, second or third. He's all very well, very original, but he's not really an all-round entertainer, more a speciality act. Somewhere, hovering around the conversation, is Halal.

"Now remember, girls, when I come back, I'm not Paul Claffey, I'm the man of your dreams..." Paul Claffey disappears offstage while the ads are playing on Mid-West Radio, then bounds back on to tumultuous applause. The music this time is the theme from 'Rocky'. Around his neck Paul has a bow tie that lights up, little yellow and red lights that flash on and off. Behind him, to the right of the stage, the spotlight picks out a towering white altar of consumer goods, the icons of the affluent society stretching fifteen feet into the air.

Copper electric kettles, microwave ovens, electric underblankets, barbecues, hoovers and boilers are stacked on top of glistening white fridges and glittering white washing machines, all topped by a huge banner proclaiming the name of the sponsor: " M. Gunning. TV Video/Elect. Equip." On the left of the stage, a day-glo sign, yellow letters on red background says "Come On Down..." On the right, a matching sign says "The Price Is Right!" Behind the stage a vast video screen, which will be used to show the items whose prices the contestants are to guess, proclaims again the name of the sponsor. Just offstage, one of the technicians holds up a sign that simply says "Applause".

Paul makes his way into the crowd to pick out four contestants."Don't be hiding, don't be embarrassed. We have spectacular prizes." He calls out numbers which correspond to those on big yellow stickers that everyone has been given on the way in: 537, 29, 751, 824. As the contestants gather he shakes a tube over each one and they are showered with coloured party streamers. Ushering them onto the stage, he keeps up a steady stream of patter. "Anything up here you fancy besides myself? My mother said I was good-looking. Am I?" And the crowds roar back "No". "If you folks at home could see me, I look fabliss: white suit, yellow tie, purple shoes. Don't I look fabliss?"

Mary from Dunmore, Margaret from Carrick, Catherine from Castlerea and Michael, also from Castlerea, line up facing the audience. It is Michael's last night in Ireland before he emigrates to New York.For Catherine, too, it is a special night - this particular weekend is a bank holiday in England, so her husband is home for a few fleeting days with herself and her children. In this setting, the domestic appliances that flash upon the video screen watched by a thousand pairs of eyes have a peculiar poignancy, acting as images of domestic bliss and harmony that for many in this crowd full of emigrants who are weekend trippers in their own town are as evanescent and taunting as a game show prize. Paul Claffey knows that the audience he is facing is one that needs dreams. "I keep the admission charges for the show down to £2.50 because I have to. If they had the money, there's no better man to get it out of them than me, but they haven't."

Mary is the first to go out when she guesses that a Zanussi washer-drier would cost £1,365. "It's about time," says Paul, "I put a bit of culture into this ignorant game." A massive sow and ten bonamhs flash up onto the screen, rooting around in a pen. For a minute or two a thousand people in their Sunday best sit in the dark and watch eleven pigs nosing around while the contestants guess how much they would cost. Michael's guess of £550 is the furthest off the mark, so he goes out of the game."Sure, what would you know about pigs and you from the town of Castlerea? Tell all on Seventh Avenue we said 'Hi' from the Midas."

Even though Margaret and Catherine knew a lot about the price of pigs, Paul greets the arrival on screen of an outfit from Chic Boutique, Castlerea, with the remark that "Now, girls, this is genuinely something that you might know something about." Again, the image is of family togetherness, the outfit described as being "ideal for a wedding or a special occasion." After this round, only Catherine is left, which means that she gets to pick a number for a prize. Paul urges her to consult her husband, he shouts up for a number and they win (drum roll, fanfare, huge cheer) a microwave oven. The band plays 'Congratulations'. "You must be thrilled," says Paul. "No need to cook his dinner now, just pop it in and press the button." He doesn't know that these days Catherine's husband has his dinner in England. Outside, in the early hours of Monday morning, something is already stirring at the factory and the sweet, over-rich smell of flesh and offal and hide is already hanging in the darkness.

119

By eleven in Halal, some of the men who were at the Midas until the small hours are already into double figures, slitting sheep's bellies, peeling back the skin so that the head hangs curiously upside down detached from the body that is already on the way to becoming a commodity, pulling out the guts with their hands and putting intact stomachs into a great vat on wheels with all the other stomachs. The pace is hectic, though methodical and matter-of-fact, but the sights are nonetheless strange: men stamping flesh with little blue harps like official documents, men loading vast rows of carcasses on hooks into cavernous trucks, men, on this May day, working in woolen hats,thick blue jackets with big padded gloves, their faces appearing eerily out of the ice-room fog, their feet planted on thin layers of iced-over concrete. And all, after a night of country and western and American game shows, working away in the name of Allah.

Down the road, in a tiny room at the back of the Midas, Paul Claffey is already back at work, hosting his regular morning show on Mid-West Radio. On his sound desk is a trophy made by a local business to be given away to the winner of yesterday's Cow Plop Contest in Bekan, a few miles away on the road to Claremorris. The trophy has a cow on the top and a large round cake that looks like cow-dung on the bottom. "Still trying to find out exactly what happened at the cow-ploppin' yesterday. If you won the contest ring us and collect this fabulous award...In the meantime, here's one from Barry Manilow." The Cow Plop Contest was one of the main attractions at the Bekan Family Day whose delights also included Ladies and Gents Tug-O'-War, Guess the Weight of a Sheep, Hammer the Nail, Throw the Wellington and Best Dressed Dog. For the Cow Plop, a field is marked out in numbered squares, each entrant is given a number and the one which corresponds to the square in which the cow first defecates wins £250.

As the morning progresses, there is more urgent business. "There's a dog missing from the Toureen/Kilkelly area, a black smooth-hair collie with a white front leg. Answers to Simon, missing since Friday." There is the No Belly Award for Paul's Plumps, women trying to lose weight. "Please don't be angry with me," writes one who has succumbed to temptation, "as I just couldn't bear it! I feel so bad as it is, after letting you down." There are items for sale: "a large dress with beaded pearls, size 14", "a fast tanning sunbed, little used". There are quizzes - "What is in every house, has a key to open it, and is made in Tubbercurry?" There is a woman who has seventy-seven Calvita tokens for a trip on the B&I and wants to sell them. There are greetings for girls home from England for the weekend. And there are songs. One of the most requested is Red Sovine's 'Teddy Bear', about a trucker "on the outskirts of a little Southern town" who gets the voice of a little boy on his CB. "I get lonely and it helps to talk/'Cos that's about all I can do/I'm a cripple, you see, and I can't walk...Dad used to take me for rides when he was home/But I guess that's over now he's gone."

Another of the most popular records is 'The JCB Song' sung by Seamus Moore. It's popular because, in the way that such songs used to mention every town in Tipperary or Mayo, it gets a long list of the pubs in Camden Town into its chorus: The Galtee, Nelly's, The Bell, The Crown...In the same room where it is being broadcast, the one with the pictures of the Pope, Louise Morrissey and T.R. Dallas on the walls, Brother Gregory stood the previous night. He teaches in the Marist Brothers in Castlerea and is director of the Castlerea Musical Society. He was talking enthusiastically about his last production, 'Guys and Dolls', less so about the increasing difficulty of finding enough young people to make up the cast. The door opened and his face brightened. In walked a young man of around twenty, his star dancer, one of the great hopes for his next production. "I'm delighted to see you," he said, "I've just the part for you..." The young man looked at him as if he were touched. "What? Me? Don't you know? I've been in London for the last six months. I'm only here for the weekend. I'm not here at all."

Magill, July 1988

121

EMIGRATION

I
Emigration: A guarantor of continuity

Like Oscar Wilde who said he could resist everything except temptation, we are, I think, a people who can adapt to anything except change. Reading the Cork "Evening Echo's" devastating survey of young people's attitudes to emigration reminds us again of the fatalism which impels us to accept anything, any amount of dislocation and disruption rather than face up to real and fundamental change at home.

Almost all of the young Corkonians see their future as bleak. But equally, most of them think of their way to avoid that bleakness in terms of escape, of emigration to a wide variety of places, from Austria to Australia. Irish young people, it seems, are prepared to put up with any amount of personal discontinuity rather than contemplate a radically altered future in their own country.

One of the things this should teach us is to stop using the word "conservative" about ourselves. We are not a conservative people; we are a fatalistic one. If conservatism means anything it is about holding on to traditional values, maintaining a way of life, keeping in touch with whatever you perceive to be your roots. And in this sense we are not an overly-conservative people, but a feckless and profligate one.

We will give up anything, adapt to any new circumstance, if only we are allowed to live in peace and comfort. We will tolerate anything short of the utterly intolerable. If Ireland was invaded by Martians tomorrow, it wouldn't be long before we started wearing antennae and telling each other that the Martians weren't such bad fellows, so long as you didn't get on the wrong side of them.

I was, for instance, in Ballyhaunis, Co Mayo, a few months ago. Ballyhaunis is the essence of what we would think of as conservative small-town Ireland, the usual huddle of buildings on the main street invaded and enclosed by the surrounding countryside. It is monumentally stable in its politics and overwhelmingly against abortion and divorce. And yet when you look at the way people live, not only is it not conservative, it is a positively surreal mixture of cultures and influences.

Most of the town's workforce spend their days in the Halal meat factory where mullahs (real live Middle Eastern Islamic mullahs) intone Koranic prayers over the beasts which are to be slaughtered. There is a mosque at one end of the town. In the Midas Nite Club on a Sunday night, the main entertainment is a live Ballyhaunis version of a British version of an American game show called "The Price is Right", compered by a man in a bow tie that lights up in pink and yellow. For the Irish emigrant, New York probably seems by comparison a model of cultural orthodoxy and cohesion.

What sustains this ability to adapt to almost anything is fatalism. Irish fatalism is peculiarly paradoxical. It is the element of continuity which allows us to accept almost any discontinuity. The continuity comes in accepting that things are rotten here and will always be rotten, and if you accept that then you put up with all the disruption that emigration brings. And even more ironically, emigration itself is a big factor in establishing that continuity. The thing which causes so much and such painful change in our individual lives at the same time convinces us that change itself is really impossible.

It does this because of its very persistence. While all has changed in Ireland over the last 150 years, emigration, except for a brief period in the Sixties, has remained the same. Furthermore, this has been very useful politically. Fianna Fail in particular is dedicated to great national goals, to the idea that there are aims, which, once accomplished, will constitute the party's final meeting with destiny.

Now in recent years these great aims - national unity, the revival of the Irish language, economic self-sufficiency - have become more and more nebulous and less and less useful as rallying cries to the faithful. What has taken their place is emigration.

In 1967 Charles Haughey was able to announce that "emigration is gone". Ending emigration, he said, was Fianna Fail's great achievement of the 1960's. But now, with the return of emigration, a great rhetorical device has returned. Fianna Fail, says the Taoiseach, banished emigration in the 1960s and "to eliminate it again from Irish life will be our objective in the Eighties".

Thus, and only thus, the Fianna Fail of 1988 is the same as the Fianna Fail of 1958. The party remains the same, its integrity of purpose is assured. National unity may be unattainable, the revival of Irish a bad joke, economic self-sufficiency jettisoned 30 years ago, but in emigration there is still one Great National Goal which has emotional and rhetorical power. In Irish political life, emigration is a guarantor of continuity.

123

We will never even begin to face up to emigration until we stop taking a certain surreptitious pleasure in it as the one thing which unifies us as a nation, which establishes our continuity with our ancestors and our history. There is a fitting symbolism in the fact that last night the nation was momentarily unified in watching a soccer team composed for the most part of the sons and grandsons of the Micks and Paddies and Marys and Brigids who took the cattle boats to the Gorbals and Cricklewood and Coventry and Liverpool in the Thirties, Forties and Fifties.

At some deep level we still see emigration as the badge of our identity at a time when we have lost so many of the other marks by which we identify ourselves. You can turn your wounds into special stigmata, but they are still, after all, wounds. Or, as Charles Haughey has so eloquently put it "acceptance of emigration as a normal feature of our national life is the ultimate in defeatism".

The Irish Times, November 1988.

II

Strangers in their own Country

I keep coming back to emigration and I know why. I and people of my generation belong to a quirk in Irish history, a flaw in the otherwise perfect pattern. We are the only generation since the Famine which has not emigrated in large numbers. Most of our friends of 10 or 12 years ago are still around, our network of friendship and knowledge and comfort is still in place. We can still walk down Grafton Street on any weekend and be sure of meeting at least one person we know, be reassured that the world of our youth is still there, dressed, perhaps in more sober style and smelling faintly of baby puke, but there all the same. Now and then, another little limb of this body of known friends is lopped off, and we find ourselves making phone calls to Illinois or writing letters to Paris, but the body still works, its blood still circulates. And when people fix us with that pitying glare and ask, "Have you ever thought of getting out?", the way a despairing teacher asks the charming class jester, "Have you never thought of opening a book?", we still don't really understand what they mean. We are at home here.

It is hard now to remember the glow of satisfaction that

surrounded those of us who came to consciousness between Woodstock and the second oil crisis. There was a real sense then, that we were the terminus of a whole era of Irish history, that we were the reward for which all those sacrifices had been made. At last the struggles of history had borne fruit in a generation of young Irish people who didn't have to go, who were free to stay and build a life in their own country. It worked on two levels. On a historical level, we made sense of 1916 and the Tan War and the bitter privations of the Fifties, proved that all of that had a point. And on a personal level we made sense of our parents' lives, balanced out all the things they had foregone, all the extra hours they had worked, all the times they had bitten their lips for the sake of their kids.

They were not to know that they were breeding a generation of freaks, a generation that believed in fantastical things like staying more or less where you were born, like having kids whose accents and manners and culture would be in a continuous line with your own, like the mad notion that if you didn't like your society, you could change it. They were not to know that they themselves would again be the real victims of emigration, that while their younger kids would be happy to go, they themselves would be the ones robbed of the happy ending that was supposed to make sense of their lives, denied the future that was supposed to make the sacrifices worthwhile.

As a member of that generation of freaks, I keep turning over that basic question of why it is that emigration, which was virtually unthinkable for the people with whom I grew up, had become, for people only three of four years younger, something that you didn't have to think twice about. The basic answer, of course, is economics, jobs, the long decline which has followed the 1979 oil crisis. It's not that it's the wrong answer, just that it's an insufficient answer. Belgium or Britain, for example, have had very high unemployment, but there was no British or Belgian diaspora in the 1980s. There is something particular about Ireland that makes us respond in this particular way to economic recession. And, more and more, I find it hard to dismiss the idea that one of these particular things is the sense of internal exile, the sense that Irish people feel less and less at home in Ireland, that Ireland has become somehow unreal, unrecognisable.

This is subjective territory - there are no statistics on the sense of unreality, no ERSI reports on whether we recognise ourselves in what we see around us - and I can only rely on experiences and memories. Two memories give the sense of what I mean. One is of a winter's night in the mid-1960s, coming home from town on the bus with my mother. We got off the bus on the main road and made our way across the canal bridge that led into our corporation estate. When we crested the slope of that hump-backed bridge, we saw, or rather did not see, an extraordinary sight. There was an ESB strike, and the estate was in complete darkness. Not only that, but there was also a thick smog, made worse by the fact that their coal fires were all that people could cook on.

We had to walk about half a mile to our house in this absolute stygian blackness. We could hear the voices of neighbours as we made our way slowly up one road, and we knew where we were by the sounds we heard. And when we turned onto our own road, all we had to do was to count the gates until we came to our own. I never forgot that triumphant sense of knowing the place, of how fixed and predictable and understandable it was. Here was a place that was less than 20 years old, that had been conjured by the corporation from green fields and an old quarry, and yet, compared to it, the backs of our hands were as foreign as Timbuktu.

The second memory concerns the same place, the same kind of winter's night, only 20 years later. I was living in another part of the city now, and on my way to visit my family. This time it was not darkness but light, the strange eerie light of fires burning in barrels, around which stood small groups of men, many armed with sticks, broom handles, crude clubs. I knew many of them - I had grown up amongst them - but their faces were literally distorted by the smoke and flickering flames from the barrels. They scrutinised my face and let me pass. Others, they stopped and questioned.

The men were there because of what was going on. At the primary school on our road, the school that I had gone to, they used to tell us not to buy toffee apples from the women who sold them from prams at the gate at lunchtime: they would ruin your teeth, they might not be clean. Now, the head brother had discovered that one day, the women with their prams at the gate were giving away, not toffee apples but free syringes and small packets of heroin, to the 10 and 11 year-olds coming out. It was good marketing, a free sample. For a few weeks after that, all the talk was of patrols, of roadblocks, of vigilance. Not only did I no longer know the place, but, compared to this post-apocalyptic landscape of burning barrels and neighbours turned to watchful defenders, the streets of Manhattan or the Bronx, familiar from all those crime serials, had the comforting ring of home. And even now, though the place is quiet and respectable and the kids who succumbed to the white

126

powder and the free syringes are off dying of Aids in London, I can never feel that I know the place again.

And I don't think that I'm alone in this. In one way or another, very many Irish people must have experienced this sense of the familiar becoming unknown, unrecognisable. Ireland has become so multi-layered, so much a matter of one set of images superimposed on another, that it's hard to tell what's in the picture in front of us.

I was reading recently in a fine new book called "The Dynamics of Irish Politics" about an incident in Ballyhaunis, Co Mayo, 50 years ago, a "pitched battle" between locals and the Guards that broke out when an official of the Land Commission tried to distribute land to "people from outside the distict".

Those people fought, presumably, because they knew their own place so well, because they considered it to be so truly theirs, that they couldn't bear to think of it in the hands of strangers, even though those strangers were probably indistinguishable from themselves. And what is Ballyhaunis like now? It is run by an Islamic meat factory, where Middle Eastern mullahs intone prayers from the Koran over the animals before they slit their throats. It has its own mosque. And as for the locals, well, on a Sunday night they go down to the local Nite Klub where a man in a light-up bow-tie hosts his own, live, version of an American game show, "The Price Is Right".

One of the most sad but comforting things about emigration used to be the tragi-comic figure of the Returned Yank. Sad because of the sense of loss, the incomperhension at the fact that everything was different from the way it was remembered. Comforting because that imcomprehension eased our sense of inferiority, told us that we were the ones who really knew, we were really on top of this place. Now it is we who are the Returned Yanks, looking around us and saying gee, didn't there used to be a pub there, didn't that place look different, didn't I know that guy? And like the Returned Yanks it is easier to go back to a place that is less complicated, less haunted by its own past, to get on the plane and go home to America, regretful but relieved.

The Irish Times, September 1989.

127

III

Some of our Emigrants are Happy to Go

We know what it means when 20,000 East Germans forsake their country for the west, that their homeland is a failed political entity, that East Germany is on the way out, a place that cannot survive without fundamental and perhaps traumatic change. We are less sure of what it means when twice that number of young Irish people are leaving every year, mostly heading in the same westward direction, and using the same language: freedom, opportunity, the chance to work and be rewarded for it. Or perhaps, more accurately, we don't want to know. We have developed, because of our history, because emigration has been with us for so long, ways of avoiding it, ways of not thinking about what it tells us. One of these ways is our notion that emigration is a tragedy.

The nice thing about tragedies is that they are inevitable, an act of God or fate or circumstance, unamenable to human actions and choices. All that we can do about them is weep. There is nothing inevitable about Irish emigration in the 1980s, no sense of "to Hell or America". No one was going to starve, as one might have done in the 19th century, nor was it a case, in spite of Brian Lenihan's remark a few years back to the fact that we can't all live on such a small island, of physical over-population. Contemporary emigration is a matter of choices made and decisions taken, and understanding those choices needs thinking rather than weeping, thinking about the way Ireland is and why it is so intolerable to so many of its young.

This is not to say that those choices are completely free ones, that they are made flippantly and without some degree of coercion. Of course people go because they have no jobs and no prospects. Of course some of them go because they are out of key with the official morality of Catholic Ireland, because they are separated or gay or in some way outside of the moral mainstream.

But that coercion is not absolute, and, besides, there are also many people going who are not in any real sense forced to go. I know a lot of people who have given up good jobs to go to England and America, and I've just spent some time in New York with one of them. What is disturbing in his case is not just that he made the choice to go but that, for him and for many others, that choice is so patently the right one. He was happy in New York, revelling in its energy and diversity.

128

What, I asked, about the pressure of working in America, the long hours and dog-eat-dog competition? Not at all, he said, you work longer hours, in a more competitive atmosphere in Dublin. But what about the crime, the constant undertow of violence? The only time he had felt that in the last year was back in Grafton Street on his Christmas holidays.

And that, I think, is one of the things that we don't want to face about emigration now. We want our friends and our brothers, our sisters and our children, to feel unhappy about leaving Ireland, to share our sense of loss, of impoverishment. We want them crying on the phone, feeling alien, disoriented, ill-at-ease in those American cities. We crave their grief, for in it would be confirmed all the things we want to hear: that Ireland is wonderful, that there is something unique in Irish life that no amount of money can compensate for, that those of us who are left are the lucky ones. Insist as we might that we only want their happiness, that happiness is still a kind of insult. Not wanting to be insulted, we go on calling emigration a tragedy.

We still want to think of our emigrants as being in a continuous line with all those who have left since the Famine. But in fact, in important respects, they are the exact opposite. The old Irish emigrants felt themselves in exile over there; the new feel themselves in exile over here. The old ones pined for a culture from which they felt themselves removed - Irish culture. The new ones have that feeling long before they go - the culture which they pine for and from which they feel themselves removed in Ireland is American culture. The old ones sang "Danny Boy" in Boston and the Bronx to put themselves in touch with their Irish homeland. The new ones have been singing "New York, New York" in Bray and Belmullet, while waiting for their Green Cards to come through. *The Green Card Rap* has replaced *Wrap the Green Flag Round Me, Boys* as the anthem of the true exile.

The point is that for very many young Irish people America already is their cultural and spiritual homeland. If you've seen the movies and listened to the tapes, if you've worn the jeans and eaten the burgers, then you might as well live the life. The old Irish in Hackensack and Hell's Kitchen desperately tried to appropriate their homeland through its cultural symbols - the songs, the music, the style.

The new Irish have already appropriated the symbols of their cultural homeland in the good old US of A. Stuck here, they are far from the land where their young heroes sleep. The new Irish have the same yearnings as the old Irish, only in reverse, and with the crucial difference that whereas their predecessors couldn't come home to Ireland, they can go to America.

One of the things that attracts Irish people to a city like New York is the American myth of equality, of absorption, the notion that whoever you are and wherever you come from, you start out blank, with no past, no handicaps, with the same basic chance as everyone else. It is an enormously attractive idea, and one that has some truth in it. Sitting in a Cuban-Chinese restaurant in Greenwich Village last Saturday night with people of Irish, Italian, Spanish and Yemeni origins, all of them by now typical New Yorkers, it was impossible not to be excited by this levelling mix, by the desire to immerse yourself in this melting pot.

The flaw, of course, is that New York is not a melting pot at all. It excludes and divides just as we do at home. What it does is to replace one principle of exclusion - the religious and national ones that we are used to - with a different one. We are used to divisions on national and religious lines - the Brits and the Irish, the Catholics and the Protestants - which make little sense in New York. But because of this we fail to see the much more rigid distinctions and divisions that it operates: it is a melting pot if you are Catholic or Jewish, Irish or Italian. It is not a melting pot if you are black, poor, old, very young, or a parent stuck on your own in an apartment block of bolted doors with a young baby.

Because of the melting pot myth though, we fail to see the extent to which the Irish exiles are reproducing Irish society in all its divisions over in the States. If you believe in the American Dream, then everyone we are sending to the States will have the same chance to end up rich and happy. What we don't want to face is that America is a screen on which our own divisions will be magnified. Those who have had good education and good jobs here will, in the main, do very well there. But those who haven't face a kind of misery and exclusion that is even greater than what they might have known here.

Either way, it is clear that the young Irish in America are an image of our own society, of a society that is economically unjust and culturally so much in hock to American images that it may never again be able to balance the books. Thirty years of being an offshore economic dependancy of the United States have left us with a society that is seen by an increasing number of its young people as a pale imitation of the Real Thing across the Atlantic.

That isn't a tragedy, but it is a part of the script that was written

130

when we decided that other countries would have to do our developing for us. If we're serious about wanting the emigration to stop - and I'm not at all sure that we are - then we're going to have to write a whole new script.

The Irish Times, September, 1989.

MEANWHILE BACK AT THE RANCH

Images of Ireland and America

Here are three items of news from Ireland after the end of the eighties:

Item 1: from *The Daily Star*, 30 January 1990. "Gunslinger Clint Eastwood is descended from a Lord Mayor of Dublin... Clint, hero of the Dirty Harry movies, is believed to be descended from Alderman John Eastwood, mayor of Dublin in 1679. And Clint himself is a former mayor of the seaside town Carmel, in California. But his ancestor was also a sheriff of Dublin - on the opposite side of the fence to the stubble-jawed outlaw of the spaghetti westerns."

A tentative conclusion from this news is that while all history is an invention, in Ireland the sense of the past is becoming an invented invention, refracted through the manufactured myths of the American movies. An Irish sheriff and a Wild West sheriff, the mayor of Dublin and the mayor of Carmel, California, 1679 and 1967, are all part of the same fiction, shooting it out on the main street of some eternal Tombstone.

Item 2: from *Magill*, February 1990: the first of Ireland's new commercial local radio stations to get into serious financial trouble is Radio West. It was established in Galway to the same formula and by the same people who ran a successful pirate station in Dublin called Treble-T R, playing the same diet of country and western music. But whereas the formula had found a ready audience with country people living in Dublin, it failed to appeal to country people living in the country. "It may well be," says the report "that a music policy which appealed to country people in flats in Dublin was to have much less appeal when directed at the same people on their home ground."

A tentative conclusion from this news is that even the country-and-western culture imported into Ireland from America is itself not so much an aspect of modernity as of nostalgia, a part of the dynamics of memory and displacement, of exile and yearning. When Irish people yearn for America they may not yearn for an America of the present but an America of the past, a remembered

132

America, a myth of America created by their own ancestors. The Irish country people in the city wanted to listen to country-and-western because it reminded them of their past, and that image of the past was American. The Irish country people living at home had less need for such nostalgia, for such an invented American past.

Item 3: from *The Sunday Tribune*, 25 February 1990. A film production company called Virginia Films is to hold the premiere this summer of their documentary "The Road to Inishfree" in Cong Town Hall, County Mayo. The film is a re-enactment of the filming of John Ford's The Quiet Man in Cong 39 years ago. Locals Anne Slattery and Paul Kane were hired to play Maureen O'Hara and John Wayne, playing John Ford's film characters based on Maurice Walsh's fictional characters. "The Road to Inishfree" says the report "reconstructs selected moments from The Quiet Man including the famous bicycle scene." Anne Slattery who played a latter-day Maureen O'Hara in the film hasn't seen the final product and half expected never to see it. "I shot my scenes almost two years ago but I haven't heard from the company since and I thought the film was shelved." Another actress who played in the documentary says she won't be at the premiere because she has since emigrated.

A tentative conclusion from this news is that it is not so much the past that we re-enact in Ireland but an American movie version of the past. We play out a dramatised version of someone else's dramatised version of ourselves, a drama which the actors never expect to be finished, or if it is finished, cannot expect to be around to see.

What I want to suggest is that America and Ireland represent not opposites, not a dialogue of modernity and tradition, but a continual intertwining in which far from Ireland being the past and America being the future, America can constitute Ireland's past and Ireland can invent America's future. When we deal with this relationship, we are dealing not with something final and closed, but with something obsessive, repetitive, continually unfinished, all the time renewing itself in old ways. We are dealing with the schizophrenic dynamics of memory and exile. And exile is both *from* and *to*. It is about both leaving and returning. In the imaginative geography of exile, everything is relative to everything else. The West of Ireland is West for Ireland, East for America. The American West can take on the contours of the Ireland back home, back east. I want to try and suggest some ways in which the notion of America itself is an Irish invention, the notion of Ireland an American invention. When

133

we step into this divide, we step into, not an open space, but a hall of mirrors.

The first important contradiction that I want to explore in this dynamic of exile is that between the native and the civilised. The American myth, of course, is the myth of the taming of the wilderness, the conquering of the uncivilised Indian by the civilised white man. The Irish, of course, played more than their fair part in this process. But the ambivalence comes from the fact that the Irish are not, in this dichotomy, either/or, they are both/and. They are natives and conquerers, aboriginals and civilisers, a savage tribe in one context, a superior race in another. At the same time as the West of America is being opened up, British colonial language is using the savagery of the Indian tribes as a convenient analogue for the native Irish. In 1844, an English traveller in Ireland remarks that "The murders of this country would disgrace the most gloomy wilds of the most savage tribes that ever roamed in Asia, Africa, or America." In 1865 an editorial in the *London Times* links the genocide of the American Indian with the genocide of the Irish, in a spirit of glee rather than outrage: "A Catholic Celt will soon be as rare on the banks of the Shannon as a Red Indian on the shores of the Manhattan." As the language of the Wild West and the Indian Wars becomes generalised through popular fiction and journalism - the one generally indistinguishable from the other - it becomes easy to apply this language to the wild Irish. A British visitor looking at Tuam in County Galway late in the last century thinks immediately of the Red Indians: "Not only are the cabins in this district aboriginal in build but they are also indescribably filthy and the conditions of the inmates...is no whit higher than that obtaining in the wigwams of the native Americans. The hooded women, black-haired and bare footed, bronzed and tanned by constant exposure are wonderfully like the squaws brought from the Far West by Buffalo Bill." *Punch* talks of "a tribe of Irish savages, the lowest species of the Irish yahoo." For Britain, the Irish are the Indians to the far west, circling the wagons of Imperial civilisation.

Once in America, of course, the Irish cease to be the Indians and become the cowboys. They are the Indian killers and the clearers of the wilderness. They are the mythic cowboys. Jesse James' father comes from Kerry; Billy the Kid, though known eventually as William Bonney, is initially known as Henry McCarty, son of Catherine McCarty. According to some contemporary reports he was born in Ireland, according to others New York, and the ambivalence itself is perfect. In his legend as it grows up he is a prodigious killer of Indians. He kills three Apaches in Sonora, rescues Texans from Apaches with the James gang. He takes on 20 "well armed savages" in the Guadelupe Mountains with only his six-gun and his dirk. But in reality, or as much of reality as there ever can be in this kind of legendary terrain, Billy the Kid fought not Indians but Irishmen. In the Lincoln County Wars he fought against the Murphy-Dolan-Riley ranching combine. The first murder he was charged with was that of the Murphy-Dolan-Riley sheriff, William Brady, a fellow Irish-American. And, of course, Billy himself was killed by another Irish-American Pat Garrett. In this seminal American myth the struggle of Irishman with Irishman in the New World is transmuted into a struggle of white man against native. Billy the Kid is Irish and American. His victims are Irish and Indian. The Irish are the killers and the victims, the civilisers and the wild men, the good guys and the bad guys. An important part of the American psyche, the ambivalence of the desperado as dangerous outlaw and rugged individualist, arises out of the ambivalence of the Irish in America. This is Ireland inventing America. And the Billy the Kid myth is itself crucially ambivalent. The transformation of Billy from foot soldier in an economic war into hero of the war against the Indians is an acceptance of the Irish as part of the governing American myth. But the ease with which Billy's Irish antagonists can become Indian antagonists shows how close the Irish remain to the Indians in the "civilised" mind. This tension between acceptance and exile, between being insiders and outsiders, liberates a set of images that is enormously influential on the development of American culture and therefore on the development of Irish culture.

This set of images is one which emerges always in a curiously self-referential way. It is not just in modern Ireland that the relationship with America is conducted through life-imitating-art-imitating-life. This is a feature of the Irish-American cultural construct right from the start. The whole myth of the American West is one in which life and art imitate each other with dizzying speed. Buffalo Bill's Wild West Show has cowboys and Indians re-enacting their wars as theatre almost as soon as they have ceased to be wars. Far from being the originator of a myth, Billy the Kid himself grew up in the mythological shadow of Jesse James. Theatricality, Irishness and the Wild West intertwine with abandon in the James story.

According to the legend, Jesse rode into the town of St Joseph's on Saint Patrick's Day 1882 to lead the Saint Patrick's Day Parade

135

on a stallion with green ribbons braided into its mane and tail. A month later an Irish playwright, one Oscar Wilde, was in the same town in Missouri on his American tour. He wrote in a letter from there that "Outside my window about a quarter mile to the west stands a little yellow house and a crowd of people are pulling it all down. It is the house of the great train robber and murderer, Jesse James, who was shot by his pal last week, and the people are relic hunters. They sold his dust-bin and foot scraper yesterday by public auction, his doorknocker is to be offered for sale this afternoon, the reserve price being about the income of an English bishop." The pal whom Wilde mentions, Bob Ford, the Irishman who killed Jesse then took a job with the repertory companies who were playing dramas about the James Boys, appearing at the interval to tell the story of how he shot Jesse. Jesse's brother Frank, meanwhile, got a job in another theatre company playing a cowboy in Wild West shows.

That this nexus of strange connections between showbusiness, Irishness and the Wild West is not merely an exotic aspect of frontier history becomes clear when you start to look at the way it enters American high culture in the work of Eugene O'Neill, and continues through American popular culture in the work of John Ford. The meaning of this self-conscious and intricate theatricality is the meaning of exile itself. Exile is a form of self-dramatisation, the assumption of a role, the tailoring of one's personality to an alien audience. Exile makes things that are unconscious - language, gesture, the accoutrements of nationality - conscious. It makes the exile a performer. And that performance involves ambiguity. It involves being who you are and being who you are playing. It involves, for the Irish in America, playing the white man and remembering the Indian that is left behind. And so, the notion of play-acting itself becomes an inextricable part of the Irish ambivalence, an essential image of the doubleness of the exile's condition.

Thus it is with Eugene O'Neill. In "Long Day's Journey Into Night", O'Neill embodies Ireland as an actor, James Tyrone. Tyrone's pull between his Irish past and his American present is also a pull between life and performance, between being who he is and playing who he should be in order to be accepted in America. It is a pull between being the Indian and playing the cowboy, between his son's description of him as an Irish bog-trotter and his own belief that Shakespeare and the Duke of Wellington were Irish Catholics. And the same is true of Cornelius Melody in "A Touch of

136

the Poet", forever performing like an Irish Catholic combination of Shakespeare and the Duke of Wellington, dramatising himself in his military redcoat. "Ain't he the lunatic," remarks O'Dowd "sittin' like a play-actor in his red coat, lyin' about his battles with the French." Both Tyrone and Melody are members of the savage Irish tribe appropriating the culture and the conquests of the white man. They are half-Indian, half-white man, and that division is their tragedy.

The connection between O'Neill and Billy the Kid may not be obvious but it is worth remembering that there is a similar mechanism of assimilation and rejection at work in both cases. Billy the Kid is the wild Irish savage but also the rugged White American, and in the development of his legend this tension is eventually resolved by dealing with Billy in conjunction with his father, his direct Irish antecedent, and splitting one off from the other. In Walter Wood's 1903 play on Billy the Kid it is the Kid's father who is the villian and who gets killed in the end in mistake for his son. Billy lives on, and starts a new life "where the sun always shines" in peaceful, civilised America. The savage Irish part is punished and expunged, the good American part is civilised and domesticated.

And something of the same mechanism is at work in both "Long Day's Journey" and "A Touch of the Poet". It is the Irish father who is the problem, who is blighting the lives of his Irish-American children. It is the Indian savage inside the Irishman that threatens the happiness of his children. Tyrone's mixture of meanness and fantasy, Melody's helplessly selfish dreams. For inside the Irishman is the primitive tribesman trying to get out. It is the Irishman inside that stops Tyrone from acting generously towards his family. And in "A Touch of the Poet", the Irishman inside actually gets out. A blow on the head makes Melody regress to primitive savage. His cultured voice changes back to the thick Irish brogue. His pretensions towards being a gentleman are dropped and he refers to his acquired American self in the third person, as someone else, a ghost, a dead man. All the biological pessimism in O'Neill, even in an early play like "The Hairy Ape" where it is not yet articulated in direct confrontation with the notion of Irishness, is to do with this sense of the primitive savage that lies inside the Irish-American attempt at sophistication. It is to do with the cowboy's fear that he might, after all, be just another Indian.

What is interesting about the way in which the Irish-American relationship works is that, having been put on the stage by a figure

137

who is both Irish and American, this image becomes available to playwrights who are either Irish or American. On the one hand, in an Irish play, Thomas Kilroy's "Double Cross" the British Cabinet Minister Brendan Bracken, born in Ireland but hiding his Irish background is caught in an explosion and suddenly the primitive Irishman is given the chance to emerge, speaking again in a thick brogue: "me father was wan of the lads, so he was, wan of the hillside men...Bejasus I was. I knew the treason prisoners of sixty-five."

And on the other hand, the image of the half-Indian half-cowboy is available to an American playwright like Sam Shepard . In a Shepard play like "True West" or his screenplay for "Paris, Texas", the wild brother who comes out of the desert, Indian territory, confronts the civilised brother who is settled in American comfort. Interestingly in both cases, the settled brother is involved with the equivalent of James Tyrone's theatricality, in one case with the movies, in the other with advertising. But the two brothers are halves of one whole, the tribal Indian part coming to haunt the settled, civilised part. The story is not now Irish, but it has its origins in an Irish-American dynamic, in the place where Eugene O'Neill and Billy the Kid meet. And in his play "A Lie of the Mind", Shepard acknowledges the Irish dimension of this American sense of doubleness. At the beginning of the third act of the play, Lorainne is remembering herself as a young girl dressed up in western outfits for dances, what she calls a "big Frontier Days" blowout. She immediately starts to search on a map, but she is looking, not for the frontier, but for County Sligo. She finds it and holds up the big map of Ireland on the stage. She decides to go back, even though she has never been there and knows no one in the country. "They'll know. All I gotta do is tell 'em my maiden name and they'll remember...We'll just stay for a little visit. Save on motel bills." There is, as I hope I've shown, a subterranean logic to this slide from the frontier days to County Sligo, from the American past to an invented Ireland.

Shepard's frequent use of the desert as the territory of the wild man, of social amnesia, of a force that underlies and undermines civilisation, is itself indebted to the work of another Irishman, John Ford. Of all the artists who shape this intricate relationship between Ireland and America, Ford is the most truly ambilvalent. Brought up speaking Irish and English, moving as a child between the States and County Mayo, working in his films with an invented America and an invented Ireland, Ford both embodies and formulates the tensions. He creates both an acceptable fiction of what America is and an acceptable fiction of what Ireland is and both, indistinguishably, help to mould Ireland's notion of a mythic America that is part of our own past, that belongs to us almost as a tradition or a heritage. Monument Valley and the Cong of The Quiet Man are equally aspects of Irish Romanticism, equally the invention of an Irish artist.

Ford's paradox is that he is at his most Irish in his American films, at his most American in his Irish films. "The Grapes of Wrath" may be a quintessential piece of Americana, but it is also deeply influenced by the Irish Famine. The displacement that is at work in it - a simple family thrown off their land and forced westwards to confront a class society at work - is the displacement of the Famine Irish forced out of their land and westwards into a confrontation with a class society. "The Quiet Man", on the other hand, may be a quintessential part of the Irish imaginative landscape, but it is a deeply American film, concerned with Ireland only as an aspect of the past. The hero of the film, Sean Thornton is an exile from his native land, the United States, trying to establish a place for himself in a country that is unmistakably foreign. And this paradox is carried through even more profoundly into the very landscape of the films. As Joseph McBride and Michael Wilmington have put it "There is a strange irony involved in Ford's visual metaphors for Ireland, the land of his ancestors, and the (American) West, the land of his dreams. The rocky, starved soil, which so many people fled is seen as a lush green endlessly fertile valley, and the American Dream to which they escaped is a desert valley slashed intermittently by rivers which serve only to emphasise its essential aridity." In this paradoxical manipulation of images, the American West becomes the West of Ireland, Ireland becomes the rich promised land of the American West. The dynamics of memory and exile are not denied, they are reversed.

For a time, Ford was able to use this juggling of East and West, the west of Ireland back east and the American west, to embody a kind of social optimism about the American dream. The Mayo of Ford's ancestry is both East and West - west of Ireland, east of America, and in a film like "My Darling Clementine" this ambivalence allows the coming together of east and west on a mythic level. The hero of the film, Wyatt Earp achieves his mythic status by embodying the best values of East and West. He is both rugged and civilised, both the man who comes in from the desert and the man who imposes order on the wild territory, both the individualist and the bearer of authority. This important part of America's myth of itself owes much to Ireland through Ford.

But what is interesting is that this ideal unity cannot last, that within ten years of "My Darling Clementine", it breaks down in Ford's work into the pain, uncertainty and confusion of "The Searchers". In "My Darling Clementine" Wyatt Earp is easily able to overcome the disruptive Indian who is one of his first conquests in Tombstone. But in "The Searchers" ten years later, Ethan Edwards (the John Wayne character) cannot so easily subdue the Indians because he carries the Indian inside him. The deft merging of Ireland and America in "My Darling Clementine" has become again the painful ambiguity of Eugene O'Neill, the cowboy who carries the Indian about within himself. Like a James Tyrone or a Cornelius Melody, Ethan Edwards is a man of American civilisation, the white settler community, who can never be part of that community because he retains a powerful affinity with the Indian, the savage tribesman. He has all the characteristics of a Western hero - strength, individualism, leadership ability, self-sufficiency - but he is at the same time anti-social, outlawed even. He is both hunting the Indians and intensely close to them, knowing their language, their signals, their meaning, sharing their instincts for violence and revenge. He is in other words, the perfect image of the Irish in America, both Indian and Indian-killer. The film's emotional tension depends on the whole question of sexual relations between whites and Indians, of the mixing of white and Indian blood, and that mixture is intensely connected to the relationship of Ireland and America. And in "The Searchers" that relationship has become sour. In the end, Ethan Edwards comes to the door of the white folk's cabin but cannot be admitted. He must turn and go back out into the desert, into Indian territory. The American Dream reveals its aspects of nightmare.

And it is important, too, that Ford repeats another part of O'Neill's triple connection of Irishness, the Wild West and theatricality. Think, for instance, of what Ford does with Lady Gregory's play "The Rising of the Moon" in his film version made shortly after "The Searchers". Whereas in Lady Gregory's play, a rebel about to be executed is rescued by another rebel, in Ford's version the rebel is rescued by the actors of the Abbey Theatre. A play-acted version of reality is turned into a play-acted version of play-acting. We are definitely into the hall of mirrors, where an Irish theatrical version of Irish reality, becomes an American film version of Irish theatre-as-reality and, when shown in Ireland is

140

accepted as more real than ever the original play might have been. The obsessive, pathological nature of these transformations is what makes Ford's Irish films so bad when compared to his American films. What he is about in the Irish films is trying to expunge Irish reality, to cut out the painful, ambiguous Ireland that the American Ford must carry around inside him by turning the real Ireland into a harmless fiction. In his films, Ford takes Irish fiction - O'Casey and O'Flaherty in particular and reduces it, getting rid of the ambivalence of say "The Plough and the Stars" or "The Informer", as if by reducing the ambivalence of Irish fiction the haunting ambivalence of Irish-American reality can be exorcised.

Ford's real Ireland is Monument Valley, the American desert landscape that has all the qualities of timelessness, freedom from history and social amnesia that the Irish romantic movement always sought in the West of Ireland. The desert is the ultimate absence of civilization and Ford's affinity with it is the ultimate extension of Ireland as uncivilised, free, timeless. The essential ambivalence of the desert lies in the fact that it is both wild, and therefore frightening, and at the same time an alternative wildness to the wildness of the American city. Jean Baudrillard says that "There is the same wildness in the endless, indifferent cities as in the intact silence of the Badlands...Death Valley and Las Vegas are inseperable." For the Irishman drawn to the cities of the new world but distrusting them as alien, the desert represents the perfect form of exile, wild like the cities but natural, indifferent like the cities, but splendidly so. In the cities and in Ford's Monument Valley everything human seems artificial, out of place. For the exile from Ireland, the desert is an acceptable kind of city and this is the source of its ambivalent power.

The essential Irishness of Ford's use of the desert helps at least in some measure to explain why the most powerful use of the desert in post-war western culture is that of an Irishman, Samuel Beckett, in which the desert becomes the image of the modern world, of the dislocated urban world that we inhabit. It helps to explain the way in which it is an Irish rock band, U2 who have been able to recreate Ford's mythic America largely through their use of the deserts of Colorado and Arizona as a dream landscape in their photographic images, their films "Under a Blood Red Sky" and "Rattle and Hum", their carefully worked-out Wild West costuming, and their post-apocalyptic born-again lyrics which use the desert as the image of a world after the nuclear holocaust.

And at the same time, the sense of the affinity with the Indians

141

remains in contemporary Irish culture. One of the most important Irish novels of recent years, Brian Moore's "Black Robe" plays deftly on the Irish ambivalence about native and civiliser. The novel's point of view moves between the Catholic missionary sent to Christianize the heathen Indians and the Indians themselves, a split which reflects the continuing resonance in a North American setting of the Irish connection to both the white man and the Indian. Or think of Paul Muldoon's recent poem "Meeting the British", in which the "we" of the narrative voice are the Indians but given the poem's title and situation of a meeting between the natives and the invading British cannot but include the Irish. The metaphor, again, is of the Irish as Indians and the fact that the metaphor can be used as in the poem self-consciously, ironically, playfully, suggests the strength of its provenance.

Even more striking is the way in which this connection between the Irish and the inhabitants of the desert can be used by an American writer with no Irish connections and even by the international media. Take, for example, Don deLillo's 1971 novel "Americana", a novel which very consciously revisits John Ford's territory of Monument Valley and its curious overlapping of a real and an imaginative landscape. In the screwed-up logic of the novel's narrator, there grows an identification between the West of Ireland and the desert-dweller, between the Aran Islands and the Sahara, between the Irishman and the modern equivalent of the Indian, the Arab. "Now that history has absolved me, I think I'd like to go very far away - to the Aran islands, to the Sahara, to some village high in the Himalayas. There to situate my stale body and well-paid mind against the wild dogs of nature. Sea, desert and mountain...I spin my Harry Winston prayer wheel. Or I stand above the furious sea, urbane man of Aran, spitting in my own face...Pure mathematics of the desert...All secrets are contained in the desert. Lines intersecting in the sand. Where you are and what you are. Bedouinism in all its bedpan humour. Buckmulliganism in its bowl. An Irish Arab lives in my inner ear, announcing news, weather and sport. He is Jesuit educated and wears the very best that dogma can buy." The lines that intersect in this sand are lines drawn by O'Neill, by Ford, by the Irish internalisation of the Empire's view of us as squaws living in wigwams. And these are connections, however bizarre, that can be made with ease in modern culture. In 1982, for instance, the New Zealand Truth newspaper ran an editorial after IRA bombings in London which brought the same Irish Arabs into the annals of current affairs: "While terrorism in any form, in any country, is appaling, there is something about the Irish brand - like that of the PLO against Israel - that makes Irish (or Palestinian) nationality difficult to bear among civilised people."

The Irish Arab replaces the Irish Indian, but still rides across the wild desert, far from civilised people. On a more benign level, and slightly less seriously, one might remark that Edward Said's recent reclaiming of Yeats as a great Palestinian poet in his Field Day pamphlet "Nationalism, Colonialism and Literature" is a part of the same strange sequence of connections.

Meanwhile back at the ranch there is a real Ireland and a real America, places connected not so much by myth as by profit and loss, productive investment, decisions made in boardrooms in Pittsburgh that reverberate in Castlebar, real cowboys running the country and real Irish Indians serving burgers in fast food joints in the Bronx. What I've been trying to suggest here is that an imaginative connection between Ireland and America is not a simple question of a clash between a traditional and a modern culture, but a much more complex set of cross-fertilisations in which America's cultural sense of itself is partly an Irish creation and Ireland's sense of itself is partly an American creation. And that nexus of connections is an essentially nostalgic and mythic one, nostalgic because it is concerned with an old vision of the American past, with cowboys and Indians, mythic because it has nothing at all to do with life either in America or Ireland now. We need to get out from under that myth. We need to turn the mirrors into windows.

1989.

THE SALES RITUAL
- A FABLE FOR OUR TIMES

Last week, one of the strangest little dramas of our times was re-enacted yet again on the streets of Dublin. Passing through the city centre on Christmas morning, I noticed that the queue for the sales had already formed, a little line of huddled figures in sleeping bags and deck chairs, stretching across the front of Clerys. Two days later, the shops opened their doors, and the temporary vagrants got their bargains. That evening and the next morning, the television and the newspapers duly reported their good fortune, they enjoyed their 15 seconds of fame and rode into the sunset with a 25-inch television in the saddle bag and a three-piece suite wagging its tail behind them. It is a peculiar enough ritual, but one that, like all effective theatre, has its own meaning for our society.

Those who think that the spirit of Christmas has been entirely lost should perhaps reflect that the queue for the sales is a little nativity play all of its own - a tale of homelessness with a happy ending. For four days, there is wandering in a strange land, no room at the inn (and the queues at Clerys started this year, appropriately enough, on Christmas Eve). Then the doors open, the little drummer boy does a roll, and the wise men present the rejected traveller with gold, frankincense and myrrh, or, if you prefer, a Sony Trinitron, a Sanyo video and a Sanderson sofa. The bright star of consumerism shines over the rooftops and a new year is born in just the right spirit. It is, indeed, a fable for our times.

Not least of the attendant ironies of this annual spectacle is that, being the one time when the "homeless" become visible, it is conducted in the context of the one thing from which the real homeless are most excluded - the pursuit of commodities. Every night of the year there are people sleeping outside Clerys and Brown Thomas and Switzers, but only when they are not actually homeless, but exaggerated consumers, do we really see them.

One young man queuing outside Clerys for a Sony television told the papers that he had encountered the homeless during his four nights on the streets and was glad to report that they were "completely harmless". Nobody thought to ask the people who

144

usually sleep outside Clerys or Switzers whether the presence of these annual interlopers was not, in fact, a nuisance.

What makes the whole spectacle so acceptable and indeed so heart-warming for the rest of us is the fact that the temporarily homeless shoppers, like the heroes of fairytales, do, in the end, attain home, or at least its most potent symbols - the televisions and carpets and microwaves and three-piece suites. An image of our society's excluded ones is conjured up, only to be banished again by a happy ending. Our Christmas sentimentality, which haunts us with worries about the poor and the homeless, can be forgotten.

The American writer Joan Didion has described the shopping centre as "the perfect fusion of the profit motive and egalitarian ideal" and the phase is certainly apt for the post-Christmas sales, which carry with them both the joy of greed and the illusion of equality. Things which were unattainable become within our grasp, if only we are prepared to suffer enough, or are quick enough or clever enough.

When the doors of the shop burst open, the stampede to the counter becomes the purest image available of the rat race of consumer capitalism, every man and woman for themselves, the law of the jungle let loose in the struggle for things we probably don't want but have to have. For a few mad hours it is acceptable to push and to shove, to tug and to tear, to cast aside the bonds of good manners and civilisation which temper the instincts of the free market.

The inherent message is simple and precise. We all start equal and the fittest and strongest take the big prizes while the hindmost scavenge for the remains. If you don't get the £2,000 leather suite for £500 or the £399 bed for £99.50 it's because you didn't have the perseverance, or the guts or the brains or the brute strength. If you didn't get the goodies it's because there's something wrong with you. Who says we no longer take the rituals of Christmastime seriously? The ritual of the sales is deeply felt and entirely meaningful, the perfect metaphor for the society which we are constructing.

In the last great depression, that of the 1930's, it was the cinema which provided consolation and escape. Now, in the ultimate triumph of consumerism, it is shopping. It seems to me to be no accident that the people who by and large have created shopping as we know it today in Ireland have all been touched with a feel for show business. Feargal Quinn's family was in the entertainment industry and the live lobsters in the tanks in Blackrock Shopping

145

Centre, the brightly-coloured umbrellas which, if it's raining, are held over your head as you leave a Superquinn store, are reminders that Feargal is, too.

Ireland's first shopping centre at Stillorgan in Dublin was associated with a bowling alley, the two together giving the Irish public a taste of the American suburbia which hitherto it knew best from "The Flintstones". From Pat Quinn's polo-neck to Maurice Pratt's simper, shopping has become a part of showbiz. While the real people who sold us things have disappeared - half of the 12,681 independent grocers in Ireland in 1967 have gone out of business - they have been replaced by the grocer-as-television-star.

And now we have the shopping centre as Utopia, the arcade as Arcadia. We have the Stephen's Green Shopping Centre which looks on the outside like it's made of filigreed icing sugar and feels on the inside like an artist's impression of life on the moon, a human colony enclosed in a gigantic bubble, a thriving community all to itself with its own buskers and its own police force. For a few minutes or a few hours we can be wrapped in the Big House nostalgia of the Powerscourt Centre, or enclosed in the warm Victorian embrace of Cork's Butter Market, all the time coming into contact with more and more things to buy. These are now our images of the future and the past. These, let's face it, are our temples and our cathedrals.

The Irish Times, January, 1989.

BRONCOS

Inside the Nevada Burger fast food restaurant on Westport's Mill Street, established, as the sign above the door proudly proclaims, in 1979, one wall is boldly emblazoned with the stars and stripes. Underneath the sea-blue Nevada state flag on the opposite wall is the motto: All For Our Country.

In the street outside ancient rituals are consummated. Men stand by their horses in silent gathering, watching and waiting for the first tentative moves towards a bargain. The itinerant dealers, sly red-faced conspirators, sidle round the square like hardened lechers at a convent school dance, their voices twisted with quiet sneers, hoping to spread despondency and pessimism. "What are you asking?" demands one. "Two hundred pound" answers the young man who holds the reins, snatching with relish at the expected beginnings of a bargain. But the dealer turns on his heel with a withering contempt. In an hour or two, when his quarry is weakened with waiting, he will return and negotiate.

The same games were played five centuries ago, the testing of nerve and mettle, the delight in brinkmanship, the arduous pleadings of cruel robbery and brazen extortion. Some of the old men who have no horses to sell go simply to stand and watch and occasionally to act as mediators, assuaging the bitterness and forcing unreconciled hands together to shake on a deal.

But at the far end of Mill Street, in the big flat car park, the trappings of organisation are in evidence, reminders of the fact that things have changed, that there is bigger business to be done, that the fair was revived only six years after it had died a natural death. Paddy Joe, a loud hailer in one hand, a sheaf of papers in the other, is overseeing the judging of animals in the "Colt Foals by a thoroughbred stallion" category.

In the doorway of the caravan that acts as office and canteen for Paddy Joe and his minions, sits the Queen of the Fair. Thick black hair hides her face as she stares dejectedly at the ground, unresplendent in pink jumper and blue jeans. As the winning foal is chosen and lined up beside the others who have earned the judges' approval, Paddy Joe signals to the Queen of the Fair and she disappears inside the caravan. She emerges smiling, a rhinestone tiara perched on her dark locks and walks over to pin a red rosette on the foal's bridle.

It is almost noon, and the deals are in full swing before Paddy Joe mounts the trailer to organise the official opening of the fair. From Bridge Street the girls' accordion, recorder and drum band, marshalled by a kindly-looking young nun, appears to the off-key strains of O'Donnell Abu, marching gingerly around the fresh pats of horse dung. From his trailer Paddy Joe calls for Senator Martin J O'Toole and Councillor Teddy McHale, and finally the politicians, representatives of the Irish Farmers Association and the Horse Board, assemble for their speeches. A small group of men gather to watch sceptically while Paddy Joe announces that "the horse is going through a very rough recession but if you stick at anything long enough, you'll win." In the square the intricate rituals of buying and selling continue, the dealers, who have been at work for hours, seemingly unmoved by the fact that the fair is now officially open.

Maam Cross is the kind of place where fairs were always held - a crossroads out in open country where the sheriff and taxman of officialdom were less apt to venture. Hemmed in by mountains, surrounded by light brown bog and still grey water, the gathering materialises from before first light. Sheep dogs nose under the tea caravans as the first queues form for the hot brew against the sharp cold of the morning. As the sun musters what strength it can, the four arms of the crossroads stretch themselves with cars, trailers, uneasy clots of cattle, horses, and pigs, stalls selling everything from goldfish to new boots, from dolls' houses to car accessories.

From the furthest reaches of the fair, on the road to Maam village, to the hub of activity around Peacocke's pub, restaurant, gift shop, grocery store and petrol pump, it is a mile and a half. A mile and a half spans the distance between the Old West and the New West, from where the sheep farmers of the hills have gathered to trade, carrying on huddled conversations in Gaelic, while their satanic irascible rams butt at the trailers in dumb exasperation, to where the sign in Peacocke's window welcomes members of Diners' Club International and the trophy for the best horse is awarded in the courtyard.

Here is the West of Ireland in microcosm: the ageing men on the outskirts, poor, dour and secretive in their language and movements; alienated from the dazzling white walls of Peacocke's, its bustling opulence and tourist appeal, its waiters in bow ties who

148

serve Irish Stew in plastic bowls and rum-and-blacks before breakfast.

And in the middle, at the Cross itself, the two worlds meet in a glorious anarchic cacophony, a chaos of anachronisms. Huge fearful horses bare their teeth and kick out at the stalled Toyotas, caught without a hope of moving through the crowds for another hour. A frightened cow, blind nature, crashes into a stall of new blue suits, and is lashed ferociously with a blackthorn stick. A bull mounting a cow brushes heavily against the mock leopard-and-tiger-skin carseat covers on another stall. A children's toy "SAS Series Paratrooper Sound Gun" is for sale next to a cassette labelled The John F Kennedy Memorial Pipe Band, Belfast, Plays Irish Rebel Songs and Marches. An itinerant playing Irish traditional tunes on a button accordion is almost drowned out by the Country and Western sound of Larry Cunningham singing Forty Shades of Green.

But there is no doubt which world is winning. The woman selling hob-nailed boots says that the demand is declining, while the man selling synthetic leopard-skin carseat covers reports a blossoming trade. The better ponies fetch good prices but most will end up as hobby-horses for the new rich, not as prized parts of the rural economy. And the proprietor of Peacocke's, his silver trophy in one hand, a poster advertising tonight's dance in his ballroom in the other, has the air of having everything well under control.

"A Fair Day", 1984.

C.SELF-MADE MEN

NOTHING SUCCEEDS
LIKE EXCESS

One night last month, in the cavernous hall of the RDS in Ballsbridge, Sean Kinsella's dream came true. To the roars of the crowd, Barry Manilow ripped off his shirt to reveal, stuck to his manly frame with sweat, Brian Mullin's Dublin GAA jersey. Gaelic manhood and bouffant bliss, the Dublin that is the capital of Ireland and the Dublin that is a local branch of the universal consumer supermarket, were melded together in a single living image. The previous night, as Barry Manilow ate his dinner at the Mirabeau Restaurant in Sandycove, Sean Kinsella, its owner and chef, had suggested the idea to him. And now here it was, made flesh before the adoring fans. "Brian Mullins came back and so will I," screamed Manilow. It was all there: suburban flash mixed with bootstraps self-belief; the success ethic hand-in-hand with sheer glorious vulgarity. It was the apotheosis of the Mirabeau.

When plush lounges started to replace the dingy little pubs that no longer matched the pretensions of the newly affluent Irish, a new form of potted wisdom was born. "You don't have to be mad to work here," said the little signs behind every lounge bar from Termonfeckin to Glenamaddy, "but it helps". Or "I like work, I could sit and watch it all day." Because there were jobs now, work was something you could joke about in a folksy way, something that, even while you were doing it, you could pretend not to be. Even while the cash register was chiming away, ringing in the new era of money, you could pretend that the money didn't really matter, that, of course, you weren't slogging your guts out day and night to get as much of it as you possibly could. And, whatever the slogan, each little wooden sign said exactly the same thing: "We may be making it big, but we're still the same good old warmhearted boys we always were." The pursuit of money still needed the sanction of the pretence that it was easily got and easier spent.

In the bar of the Mirabeau Restaurant, there is the biggest such sign in the world. As you drink your champagne cocktail, it hangs over head, at least five feet tall: "The management regrets that it has come to our notice that members of the staff are dying on the job

152

and failing to fall down..." Someone, you sense, is protesting too much.

In the far corner is Demis Roussos, a Greek pop singer with the voice of a strangled piglet, a man so fat that he wears tents. Roussos has a look of boundless voracity, as if he were auditioning for the part of Gluttony in a medieval morality play, as he sits, about to devour untold quantities of steaming food which Sean Kinsella is serving up, the two of them frozen forever in a flat woodcut hanging on the wall. They perch there, these two roundy men, the Mirabeau's very own household gods to whom the would-be diner must pay homage before passing into the inner sanctum of the restaurant itself.

A few minutes earlier, the door had opened to reveal the welcoming grin of Sean Kinsella, summoned from his kitchen where the copper pans are spitting and sizzling, by the elegant chime of the doorbell. A word of greeting, then our coats are spirited away, and we are ushered into the bar. Al Alvarez and his friends from the big poker game in town relax in one corner, the winners dying to spend their money, the losers dying to prove that they still have some to spend. As we sit sipping, two men bearing huge white dishes enter the room. They are probably meant to look like nineteenth century footmen. In fact, in their red tartan waistcoats, broad red cravats, flowing white shirts with billowing sleeves, and tight black trousers, they look awesomely like Foster and Allen. Suddenly, Sean Kinsella is among them and the parade begins.

"The lamb, sir," he says as you nod insanely at an enormous lump of raw red meat thrust under your nose. Fat, white, naked prawns lying on the dish like bloated blindworms; oozing bloody cuts of steak that might have come from a boxer's black eye; two whole sizzling duck, pass before your eyes in quick succession, each announced with the libidinous relish of a madam parading her girls before the customers. The room fills with embarrassed "ahs" and "mms". What do you *say* to a lump of raw flesh?

In April 1972, conspicuous consumption was not easy in Dublin. Jammetts, the Dolphin, the Russell, had all closed, their faded gentility no longer in keeping with the needs of the new rich. Sean Kinsella, chief executive chef with the P&O shipping line, returned to his native city, a local boy who had made good, and bought the Mirabeau from an ex-RAF pilot. He had ideas about selling good food simply cooked. He had ideas about staying open all night if that was what the customer wanted. But, most of all, he had a culinary secret. He knew that the smell of fresh money, crisp and clean and green, was the best appetiser in the business.

Not for the new rich of the Irish economic miracle was the intimidating formality of Continental gastronomic restaurants. Not for them the arcane intricacies of menus that were like secret passwords, knowledge of which defined the insiders, the inheritors of an unbroken tradition of moneyed culture that stretched back over centuries. There was, in Ireland, no such tradition. Things were too raw, too delicately poised between an ignominious past and a civilised future. To eat and be seen to eat, to spend and be seen to spend, to be served by a man whose Rolls Royce was glinting outside in the moonlight, and yet to be welcomed as if into a humble family home, here was an Irish solution to an Irish problem. To eat vast amounts of food, as if in expiation of the Famine, to enjoy the thrill of not counting the cost, all of this was a blissful defiance of the past, the collective past of want and fear. Sean Kinsella understood all of this. For he, too, was a self-made man.

He was born on the Clonliffe Road on Dublin's Northside, the son of a boilerman in the Richmond Hospital. At 14 he was cycling into the Gresham Hotel at four in the morning to start work on the breakfast. His mother bought the bike by installments, on hire-purchase from Hanna's in Stephen's Green. In the afternoons, he in turn hired the bike out to workmates who wanted to slip out to the bookies, charging threepence a time. Even then, he knew about money.

"Tony O'Reilly," he likes to tell people, "was the only man going to his school with an apple and when he got to the butt he sold it for a halfpenny". Sean Kinsella was willing to sell them the whole apple, and for considerably more than a halfpenny. He learned that there were people willing to pay whatever it took to make people believe that they didn't need to worry about money, and he made sure that he was there to scoop the pot.

The parade of food is over and we are shown into the restaurant proper. The tables are fixed, the seats back to back. On the walls are more garish woodcuts of famous guests — Burt Lancaster, Peter Ustinov — their presence essential to the illusion that all of this is about something international, something cosmopolitan, and not about something deeply provincial. The wallpaper is lush, flecked with deep red and gold stripes, adding more than anything else — more even than the hushed lighting and heavy-lidded concupiscence

154

of the diners faced with all this succulent flesh — to the atmosphere of the bordello. The Mirabeau is a culinary fleshpot, where pleasure is purchased in private, where secret indulgences are indulged.

As with any such place, discretion is of the essence. The *patron* never demurs where the whims of the client are concerned. When men booking tables whisper over the phone "Pretend you know me," he greets them with a special smile. When, recently, a young man, anxious to impress his companion, complained loudly that his asparagus was too tough, not realising that only the tips were to be eaten, Sean Kinsella was apologetic. "I must have undercooked them," he said. He even keeps a supply of fresh shirts upstairs for customers who have been sick over themselves. His business is entertainment, his performance always professional.

The food begins to arrive, long trays of spongy scallops, deep dishes of plump prawns, a gargantuan lobster swimmimg in an ocean of rich, creamy sauce. It is more, much more, than the greediest gourmandiser could manage, but the quantity, the opportunity for waste, the glorying in superfluity, is as important as the quality, which is real and undoubted.

At the table opposite ours, a small group of computer sales reps is choosing cigars, going the whole hog to impress the girls. "By the way," says one of the girls to another "this is Richard." "No, I'm John, he's Richard." The girls retreat to the toilet, to the Silvikrin hairspray and the cotton wool balls laid out on a white dish covered in aluminum foil. In the men's toilet, another young rep is brushing his Peter Mark tresses in front of the mirror. The bottle of after-shave beside the handbasin is open. There is a smell of Blue Stratos in the air.

Waiting for the bill at the Mirabeau is like standing at the top of a ski jump, contemplating the long unpredictable drop with a mixture of fear and excitement. Because there are no prices on the menu, and the reckoning of tallies is famously capricious, you have no idea of the cost. An innocently white piece of paper, neatly folded, is presented on a dish, as if it were a soothing after-dinner mint to aid the digestion. There is a thrill as you unfold it, a flutter as you read the figure. Two dinners and a bottle of wine — £112.85. The wine is Le Piat D'Or white, sold in supermarkets for less than £5, in one off-licence for £3.99. At the Mirabeau it costs £17.

I call a taxi and we move into the hallway. A waiter opens a door, and there, lying on the stairs, are our coats, taken with such ceremony when we came in. "Don't worry," says the waiter "these stairs are hoovered five times a day." At the door, Sean Kinsella waves goodbye.

155

Three nights later, I returned to the Mirabeau, announced now as a journalist writing a story. The press is important to Sean Kinsella, since by reporting the presence of the latest celebrity at his restaurant, journalists create the sense of conspicuousness without which the consumption is unfulfilled. For the brightest and best, the bills are often cost price, subsidised by the Unknown Patron. This time, we are shown into a different room in the restaurant, one with more space and bigger tables and a view through the window of the Rolls Royce outside. Sammy Smyth of The Sunday World is there with Aidan Hand, manager of the Furey Brothers. At another table, a man is ordering Dom Perignon. A woman is looking into his eyes.

The service is much sharper than before. Where before we saw Sean Kinsella only at the beginning and at the end, now he checks regularly that everything is to our satisfaction. There is a white wine with the first course, red wine already decanted on the table, sparkling wine with the dessert, brandy to finish off. I ask for the bill. "Not at all," says the waiter. "Compliments of Mr Kinsella." Before we leave, Mr Kinsella asks us to come back, say, for an anniversary or a birthday. He presses a bottle of wine into my hands as a parting gift. It is Le Piat D'Or white.

When the Mirabeau was invaded by the Unemployment Action Group, who marched around with placards chanting slogans for a while, Sean Kinsella felt, he says, that it was a suffocating nightmare. He believes in success and peppers his conversation with the names of celebrities he has met. He sees himself as a patriot, an unofficial ambassador for Ireland. He does not understand why people resent his restaurant. "In Ireland," he says "success is a very bad word. I think it's because there are too many cushions for people. You go to America, and someone's doing well, people say 'Let's try and do just as well.' I worked 17 hours yesterday. Most of the people who pull you down, they wouldn't work six hours. Because you want to do a job for your country as well as yourself, they say you've no business. As Patrick Kavanagh said 'A poet has no business to be successful in his own country.'"

"What are you working for? Nothing! You're working to keep those fellas going around the streets doing nothing. I think any man getting money from the state should be made to go and do something for it. I always maintain, if you want work, no matter how bad the recession, you'll get work. There's always an opening."

In a corner of the Mirabeau, on their own, sit a middle-aged man and woman, he with distinguished grey hair and grey suit, she in twinset and pearls. They have the look that says "money". They are talking about racehorses, trainers, jockeys, courses. A waiter arrives with a fat Dover Sole in a dish. "Yes," says the woman with a superior smile "I think I'll have that."

The waiter returns with the cooked food. They are still talking about horses. "Do you have anything running tomorrow, sir?" he asks deferentially. "Yes." He names the horse, to be ridden by Joe Mercer. "I lost my house on a horse once," says the waiter. "I mortgaged it for £2000. That's all it was then. I put it on at 10/1. It lost."

The couple look uneasy. Waiters are not supposed to tell you their troubles, especially not here. After a moment of silence, the woman speaks. "Was it a handicap race?" She looks at him as if he were quite the most absurd thing she had seen for a long time. "You should never put a large bet on a handicap." The waiter clicks back into his place in the order of things, and begins to serve the food. The woman sits back with a smile, glad that the momentary narrowing of the distance between the rich and the rest is over. Normality returns to the Mirabeau.

Sunday Tribune, October 1983.
(Shortly after this article appeared, the Mirabeau Restaurant closed on foot of a demand from The Revenue Commissioners for a large amount of unpaid taxes and re-opened under new management).

THE MAN IN THE ROLLS ROYCE WITH A CIGAR IN HIS MOUTH

There was not so much as a shudder from the Rolls Royce as it tucked gracefully in behind the bus which was rattling down Ulverton Road in a thick cloud of black fumes. "We'll pass it out at Glasthule," said the driver, clenching his teeth on his fat cigar, like the commander of the cavalry giving the order to head 'em off at the pass. We had wafted, in the splendour of the Silver Shadow, past Coliemore Harbour, where himself and his Da had once tried to drown their dog Jack, past the Dalkey Island Hotel, where Squinty McLaughlin, who taught him maths in the Presentation College in Dun Laoghaire and later committed suicide, used to drink alone, and on down to the bus terminus, just as the number eight was pulling out. Seemingly out of spite it sped past all the bus stops, down through Glasthule and past the Forum, where he queued every week for many years to watch the stars, from Fay Wray to James Mason.

The tour buses used to stop at Coliemore Harbour only for a brief look at Dalkey Island. Now, from his study across the road he can see the couriers point at his house as well. "And on your right is the house of the famous playwright Hugh Leonard, whose play 'Da' won the Tony Award for the best play of 1978, the Drama Desk Award, and the New York Critic's Circle Award. Mister Leonard, who was born in 1926, has a wife and a daughter." In The Club, where he drinks, Americans approach him, brandishing copies of an article about Dalkey which he wrote for the New York Times last December.

He now inhabits the same world as the film stars whose images once filled so many of his waking hours. "My mother," he says "was a terrific film-goer, and I went with her. It was Sunday, Monday and Friday down the local. We got our education there." When the Leonards moved into their present home, their first house guest was James Mason, a good friend. The other day Mike Todd rang to talk over a few details of Leonard's script for "Herself Surprised", to be filmed here shortly with Mason, Elizabeth Taylor and Richard Burton. He has written a new film script, a female version of "The Sting", for Maureen O'Sullivan and Mia Farrow.

The movie dream-world has seeped into the reality of his life. The portrait of him by Robert Ballagh that hangs in his study shows him as a mean, cool Philip Marlowe. He did once hire a private detective to try to find out the identity of his natural mother. As a girl, his wife, who is Belgian, lived for a time in California, where she auditioned for a film part and was told that the choice was between her and an English girl. At her parents' request, she withdrew from the contest. The part went to Elizabeth Taylor. The film was "National Velvet."

Like a character in one of his own plays, he stands between two worlds. The name "Hugh Leonard" is not his own. It is the name of one of his characters, Hughie Leonard, who appears in "The Italian Road", which was rejected by the Abbey. When he submitted "The Big Birthday", which was accepted, he adopted the pen name.

"It's very inconvenient now. I'm known in Dalkey as Jack Keyes, my name is John Joseph Byrne, I'm known as John Keyes-Byrne, I'm known as Jack Leonard. I let people I don't like call me Hugh. It's a real code. If there's somebody that is known to me, and people hear him call me Hugh, they just turn away and smile because they know that I'm not that fond of him."

His life and his writing are so intertwined that it was fitting that one of the most central details of his life, the fact that he was adopted, should have been revealed publicly on stage, in "Da". He was conscious of the public shock. On the opening night he made his way to the Olympia bar after the first act. The crowd was six deep, the chances of getting a drink slim. At once four men whom he had never seen before pointed to him, as much as to ask "What are you having?" In a few moments he had four Scotch and sodas in front of him. He knew the play was going well.

"My mother, whoever she was, covered her tracks with the most marvellous ingenuity. She just did not want to leave any trace of the fact that she had had a child. My mother's name was Annie Byrne on the birth certificate, and the Annie suggests a certain lack of education. People call themselves Anne or something."

As a child he was an omnivorous reader and was called "Go-by-the-wall". "Not for the usual reasons (a go-by-the-wall is defined in the glossary to his Joyce adaptation 'Stephen D' as 'a devious, sly person'). But I always had a book in my hand, feeling the wall with my elbow so I didn't have to look up. Once I could feel the wall I wasn't going to walk under a bus." He wrote his first piece at the age of nine.

"Graham Greene said that the greatest recipe to be a writer is to have an unhappy childhood. I would say probably, but I would correct that or enlarge it to say a solitary childhood. I had a more or less solitary childhood because I was an only child, because I was adopted, and because I was a bit of an oddball in the sense that I was very creative and very anti-sports. When you're apart and left to your own devices then you're inclined to write and create your own world if the outside world isn't to your liking."

In the Civil Service, a whole generation was "doing a line". When he entered the Land Commission in 1945 at the age of eighteen, he earned £3.14s a week. Most could not afford to marry on such wages. His job was sending out warrants for defaulters, his most intelligent task was writing a letter. He lived in dread of the foul humours and bitter wit of his superior John T. Mulligan, known in "Da", "A Life" and "Home Before Night", Leonard's autobiography, as Drumm. He refused to take the promotion bar examination because he was afraid his salary might increase too much and make it impossible to leave.

When he did leave in 1959 his wages, with a wife and child, were £10.8s. Already, writing for radio serials was bringing in a steady £33 a week. He had joined the Lancos dramatic society in the Land Commission and begun to act (he was good in comedies, terrible, he says, as Joe Keller in 'All My Sons'), direct and eventually write plays. Mark Grantham, an American who was writing 'The Kennedys of Castleross', asked him to take over some episodes. Soon he was writing that and two other soap operas for radio. Each episode took two and a half hours to write after work in the evening.

A year later he was in Manchester, working as a script editor for Granada Television and moonlighting for other television companies, writing for slots like "Armchair Theatre". Over the next decade he would, from his new house on Barnes village green near London, and with the help of a new agent, Harvey Unna, become one of the most important figures in British television. He worked with speed, efficiency and a technical mastery that was outstanding. He did adaptations of works by other writers, from Dickens to Dostoevsky, an episode in two days.

He wrote original television scripts in six to eight weeks, everything from "Insurrection", RTE's commemoration of the fiftieth anniversary of the 1916 Rising ("There were a few things that RTE would not let me do. They would not let me mention the fact that Pearse had a squint. They would not let me mention that de

160

Valera's nerves were shot and he became quite hysterical. The warts were removed by order. It would have been extremely wrong of me to impose my own views or to make personal statements"), to "Me Mammy", the Milo O'Shea serial which poked fun at Irish Catholicism. Already, in 1962, he had made the West End with "Stephen D". Every year he took three months off to write a play for the Dublin Theatre Festival.

The Dramatists Club met three times a year in the Garrick Club. Robert Bolt and Harold Pinter, Robert Morley and Wolf Mankowitz, Keith Waterhouse and Hugh Leonard ate their dinners and got drunk. Once, Leonard wrote "bollix" in the historic records book of the club after the signature of another playwright. Once he objected when Robert Morley referred to him as an Irish Catholic, allowed Morley a flustered speech of apology and then said "I am." Once he was leaving with Harold Pinter, who had just been decorated by the Queen, and Pinter complained that not one of the others had congratulated him on his award. Leonard apologised - it had slipped his mind. "Oh no, I didn't mean you," said Pinter "I know you're all right. It's the others...."

"If you do a hit play every year and if you pack the Olympia or the Abbey for six weeks, you stand to make about five thousand pounds, which, face it, isn't very much. So your plays have got to go abroad to make money and to support yourself in that sense. Irish plays go abroad very, very rarely, because they're regarded as 'Irish plays', that is as something very different from the normal run of plays, something quaint, but one cannot identify with them. In America, if an Irish play fails, suddenly Irish plays are out. Nobody takes chances. Friel's play 'Freedom of the City' lasted nine days in America and at once there was no hope of getting 'Da' on in America for another two years."

His influences, he says, were O'Casey and Lennox Robinson all right, but much more so Kaufman and Hart (authors of "The Man Who Came to Dinner"). "They knew how to make a play work. Construction in a play is most important." His two major Irish contemporaries, Brian Friel and Tom Murphy, are close friends of each other's, not of Leonard's. Tom Murphy, he says, is "the best writer on Irish provincial life, but when he gets intellectual his plays become turgid. I hate 'The Morning After Optimism', but then I love 'The White House'."

To a degree, he feels similarly about Brian Friel. "I think Friel's plays have been coloured by his attitude towards the North and his need for incorporating nationalism. Political plays are usually very

161

boring plays. Friel's play 'Translations' has been accepted by the British press as being about the roots of the Irish troubles. I think the message is much simpler. It's 'Brits get out'."

Leonard was literary editor of the Abbey in 1976 and 1977. "They asked me for a report on my work, and in the course of my report I said that the play editor, which was me, should be allowed a vote on the acceptance or rejection of a play, not as a piece of power, but as a responsibility, since he was the one who was pushing the play. They turned this down totally at a meeting. There was a leak from the meeting, and Tom Murphy made some remarks about why I had taken the job and I heard those remarks, and then I heard about the first night of a play by Tom MacIntyre, when Brian Friel and Tom Murphy got a bit tight and they were shouting 'We're gonna get Leonard out of the Abbey.' They were shouting it in the pub. My reaction was: no need to worry about getting me out. I'm gone." At the Abbey's request he stayed in the job until the end of the year and then resigned.

"I haven't seen Brian Friel for about ten years. Our paths just haven't crossed. He gets in a newspaper and he says this, and he gets in a bar and he gets tight and he says that, and he doesn't seem to realise that there's room in Ireland for more than one playwright. I think the curse of Irish playwrighting is that it's been parochial for years and this is why Irish plays have no validity outside. They don't write about men, they write about Irishmen."

He writes plays for himself, but he is himself a different brand of Irishman to his theatrical contemporaries. His exile was not cunning and far from silent. It was a golden ladder. Charlie Haughey brought him back in 1970. The tax exemption for creative writers, symbol of the brash, materialistic, brand new island of scholars if not saints, made it more attractive to live here and gave him more time for writing stage plays. He became the playwright of a new Ireland, the Ireland of social mobility to which he himself emphatically belongs.

"I have an accountant who has invested whatever money I have. I bought a boat recently. We live so modestly that we don't need the money very much. I meet my best friend in the pub on Monday night. I go out again on Friday night, which I don't like because the pub is crowded, but my wife likes to go out socially on Friday night. Sometimes on Saturdays we play penny poker - sometimes we to down to the boat. I hire videos and play them rather than go to the cinema nowadays. We go out a lot, but not far away, not to town. I like to travel a bit. I go to Greece a lot and New York when I can."

"I lived abroad for such a long time and became fascinated by the movement of society here. In another country you can see a society on the move very, very gradually because it's such an intricate and a confused process. Here you can see people with one foot in the old world, one foot in the new world. And as I once said an Irishman still believes that a rich man can't get through the eye of the needle. But now we've got the money to build bigger and better needles."

When the Leonards returned to Ireland, it was firstly to a house in Killiney, on a new estate of the sort P.J. describes in "Time Was": "It's the kind of neighbourhood where no one shouts. In fact Ellie has to give herself a home perm before she puts out the dustbin. Pathetic." He, the gardener's son from Kalafat Lane, was in among the nouveau comfortable.

"When we moved back here we were living in Killiney in a place known to the locals as Disneyland. The people there, mostly fairly well-to-do and a few chancers, were so insecure living in this new milieu that they were almost afraid to talk to their neighbours because each one said 'I'm a phoney. I don't belong.' And you had a whole estate of imposters, including myself really because we were just looking for a house and this was the only one we could find."

The nouveaux riches are not the stuff of tragedy. They have no real aspirations, only fears of a return to where they came from. (Ellie in "Time Was" complains "People spend half of their lives gathering a few nice bits and pieces together to make a house livable, and the other half sitting at home in case someone steals them.") There is no heroic possibility in them. The only drama of their lives is its schizophrenia. Hugh Leonard writes about them as no other Irish playwright could. "They are enjoying a much better kind of life," he says "but they are still anchored in the past. There's a kind of guilt about being relatively well off when your parent's weren't."

A few years ago he opened a fashion show in the new sports stadium in Dalkey. He describes the audience in "Home Before Night": "From the relative luxury of their present world they could afford to look back with an affectionate longing for the one from which they had escaped. The high point of that evening was a display of swimsuits, wispy nightdresses and couture as haute as one would find the length of Grafton Street. A few whoops of mock horror went up - this was, after all, Dalkey. But I thought of my mother in the kitchen of our house not fifty yards away, and for a moment she was alive again and looking out of the back window and through the stadium wall, and I heard her again asking my father what the world was coming to."

"If I book first class on a transatlantic flight," he says, "which I do so I can sleep, I always feel a bit guilty. It's the old granny in kitchen thing, and I say 'Christ, Leonard you do like your comfort' and things like that. You're the first to despise yourself for certain actions before others get a chance."

Of his 1971 farce "The Patrick Pearse Motel" he says "It's an attempt to bridge the two worlds, the worlds where you have one foot in your granny's parlour and wakes and things and the other foot up in Foxrock and your g and t's on a Sunday morning."

His most famous play, "Da", dramatises the conflict between his own past and present. The autobiographical Charlie returns home from England to attend his father's funeral. He is haunted by the memories of his childhood and the figure of his Da. He had failed to buy off his past life with money. "Since I was born, 'Here's a sixpence for the chairoplanes, a shilling for the pictures, a new suit for the job, Here's a life.' When did I ever get a chance to pay it back, to get out from under, to be quit of you?"

In the business of commercial theatre, the most successful plays are plays about its audiences. Leonard offers up, seasoned with laughter, images of bourgeois insecurity and impotence. Deprived of a real sense of themselves, his characters are fighting to stand still. In "Summer" and "The Patrick Pearse Motel", for instance, they lust for sex or new experience, but they are firmly wedded to their safe existences. For coherent ties with the world, they substitute individual moments of excitement. Speaking of her husband, Grainne in "The Patrick Pearse Motel" says "he is so bloody dull, and this house is dull, and I would love to have a man just once, just once before my throat gets wrinkles and people look at my brooch first and then my ring, and then me, and I swear, I swear I will never ask for another thing as long as I live - just one short fleeting night of harmless innocent adultery."

Leonard's people are powerless to change, or at least they have convinced themselves that they are. In "A Life" Drumm's perception of himself and the world changes, but only because he is dying. Leonard's best play, and the one of which he is proudest, "Summer", most clearly expresses this view of the world. "One day," he says "I said 'I'm forty-six, O Christ, I'm going to die.' I didn't have an immediate sense of dying. I just had a sense of mortality. I said 'I am coping with this by trying to write better. How are other people coping?' And so I wrote 'Summer' out of this, without ever mentioning that they had this awareness."

The eight people in "Summer" are all at various grades of middle-class life, are all locked into inescapable impotence. They have no sense of destiny in the world or of continuity in history. They are moving steadily towards death. "They were like characters sitting on a tram," says Leonard. "Some couldn't wait to get to their destination because they'd go to heaven. Some screwed on the journey because it took their minds off the destination. Some got out and picked flowers and got back on again. But everyone reacted in a certain way to the speeding-up process."

Leonard is amused by the spread of adultery as the new pastime of the middle-class. "Walking into a local pub on a Friday night where you can actually cut the vibrations with a knife is very entertaining." In "Summer" we see three married couples, first in 1968 and then in 1974. Richard and Jan have passed the intervening years in an adulterous affair. Between the two acts they have aged physically, as time wreaks its destruction on their flesh. Sex is a means of suspending time and finding a union with the world. But the flesh is a reminder of the dominion of time and of man's decay. Leonard's people have no union with the world, no class or nationality, no history. Sex is powerless to stop the tram for them. Richard understands this: "It takes so many years and you do so much harm before you own up to it that in your whole life there is you and there are strangers and there is no one else. There's a clock in the room, and you invite people in for drinks, and hope the chat and the laughing will drown out the noise of it. Well, it doesn't and after a while you realise that they're listening to it, too. You wish they'd go home."

In "Time Was" the neurosis is made tangible on stage. The past irrupts into the present as the dreams and fantasies of yesteryear slip through a disjunction of time to assault two middle-class couples. P.J., whose memories materialise, could well be Hugh Leonard. He is obsessed with old films, he has a house in Killiney and out of his past is conjured up a prostitute called Tish who used to hang out by Dun Laoghaire pier and who makes an appearance in "Home Before Night". The play is a comic nightmare, the cheap fantasies of the past catching up with the empty luxury of bourgeois life. For P.J. real experience, genuine sensation, exists only in his memory. He tries to conjure the image of his wife as she was when he fell in love with her first. He cannot resolve the past and the present, so he disappears into the past.

The impulse of Leonard's work is not to confront the world, but to shore it up. There is no rejuvenation in the laughter, only comfort.

There is quarrelling but no quest. There is resignation but no resolution. His characters find solace in accepting their own impotence. "Summer" ends with the couples still locked in their time capsule but dancing foolishly while the younger actors clap their hands. In "A Life" weakness brings its own reward. Drumm's wife wins out because she understands and plays on his contrariness, not because she confronts it. Of the opening night of "A Life", Leonard remembers "I could see the audience in the Abbey. They were all leaning forward slightly in their seats towards the end of the play. It was as if they were saying 'There had better be an answer in this or else I'll tear up the joint.'" The play provides an acceptable answer. The audience goes home happy.

In Dublin, September, 1982.

GAY BYRNE

Voices From the Silence

The man sipped, replaced his pint on the bar counter and glanced through the haze of cigarette smoke at the television screen. The shot on the screen moved from a close-up of Gay Byrne's face to a wide view of the audience. The man froze for a moment, then grabbed his coat and pushed furiously through the doors onto the street, leaving his half-finished pint on the counter. Back in the pub, Gay Byrne's voice continued to mingle with the Saturday night chinwag, with the passion and the trivia, with the vital questions of the day and the chit-chat that would not outlive the night.

A short while later in Montrose, the Late Late Show audience was streaming out into the pouring rain. Many were sheltering under the colonnade in front of the studio when they heard the screams. The security staff heard them too and rushed to Montrose House, just across the grounds from the studio entrance. There, on the steps of the old house, they found the man from the pub brandishing a knife, threatening another man while a woman screamed. The man with the knife had seen something he did not expect to see on the Late Late Show: his wife in the audience with another man.

He had suffered a more extreme version of the things that had outraged, delighted, entertained and disturbed Irish people since Gay Byrne began to present the Late Late Show in 1962: the revelation of intimacies in the glare of the studio lights, the disclosure in public of things that had never been disclosed in private. For once, that wet winter's night, the show outside the studio was brasher, more dramatic and more spectacular than the one inside.

Gay Byrne's extraordinarily central place in the Irish life of the past three decades is due, not to his own obvious skills - the flow of language, the plausibility, the urbanity - but to their oppisite: to the culture of silence which surrounds them. "I have never," the letters to him say," told this to anyone in my life..." "I feel very depressed at times and wish I could reveal my secret to somebody..."

"That was ten years ago and since then my mother and I have never mentioned it... Please don't use my name or address as I couldn't stand it if the neighbours knew..."

It is the silences that have made Gay Byrne what he is in Ireland: the silences at the breakfast table, the silences around the fireside, the silences on the pillow. Without them he would be what he so patently is - a superbly professional broadcaster, confident, adaptable, quick thinking and fast talking - and no more. With them, he is something else altogether: the voice in which the unspoken can be articulated, the man who gives permission for certain subjects to be discussed. He is the voice, calm seductive and passionless, in which things that would otherwise be unbearable can be listened to, things like this letter which he read on the radio in February 1984: "When I learned that the thing that happened between men and women, as it was locally known, had happened to me, I slowly realised that I might also be going to have a baby... In terror and panic, I tried to find out from newspapers any snippets of information. I learned that babies like the one I might have were usually placed in brown paper bags and left in a toilet and I resolved to do this... For that reason, I started to carry around the one penny I would need to get into the toilet to have the baby... I kept the brown paper bag in my schoolbag and kept the bag under my bed at night... Since I spent most of my time in the chapel praying, the nuns told me I had a vocation."

Surrounded by that silence, we wanted, in the 1960s, to hear ourselves speak in a charming, sophisticated and worldly-wise voice. And here was a man who had made it in England with Granada TV and the BBC but still wanted to come home, a man who could talk on equal terms with suave foreigners and still be one of our own, who could mention sex and nighties and contraceptives and still be a good Catholic. It is significant that the thing most frequently said about Gay Byrne's broadcasting style, by himself and by others, is that he asks the questions that the audience at home would want to ask but wouldn't dare. His achievement is founded on Irish people's inarticulacy, embarrassment and silence, on speaking for us because we were - and to a degree still are - afraid to speak for ourselves.

If we're too embarrassed to have a national debate about contraceptives, the Late Late Show will do it for us. If we're too shy to harass the fellow who sold us a dud washing-machine, the Gay Byrne Show will harass him for us. If we're too ashamed to tell our friends that our husbands haven't spoken to us for 20 years, Gay Byrne will tell the nation for us. And however much pain may go into such letters, just hearing them read in that smooth, warm, sophisticated voice already transforms the pain into something cool and clean and modern, into another masterly performance. We have been, literally, making a show of ourselves, with Gay Byrne as the cast of thousands.

His presence is now so all-pervasive that it is easy to forget that the first star of the Late Late Show was not Gay Byrne but television itself. Gay Byrne has explained that the initial idea for the show was that its ambience should be that of an evening around an Irish country fireside with the young master entertaining his guests. The image was one out of de Valera's Ireland, out of the lexicon of the man who had opened RTE itself a few months before the Late Late Show went on the air as a temporary stop-gap.

What de Valera had imagined television to be like was made clear in that opening address. He saw it as presenting "the good, the true, the beautiful": "the masterpieces of architecture, engineering, sculpture, painting... the great musical compositions of the great composers". "I find it hard to believe," he said "that a person who views the grandeurs of the heavens, or the wonders of this marvellous world in which the good God has placed us, will not find more pleasure in that than in viewing, for example, some squalid domestic brawl or a street quarrel." But Gay Byrne didn't present the Late Late Show as cosy fireside chat. On the contrary, and long before it became the fashion in television elsewhere, it went out of the way to make television itself a star, showing the wires, the lights, the monitors, the cameras, the technicians, and, of course, the hero of the hour, the audience.

It celebrated television as the very image of modernity, of technology, of all the things we were trying desperately to become. And as it went on, it filled itself with domestic brawls and street quarrels, with battered wives and Bernadette Devlin fresh from the barricades, presenting the good, the true and the beautiful only insofar as they added to the mix, kept the audience amused and the TAM ratings up. If the Gay Byrne who was doing this had not existed, he would most emphatically not have been invented, for the Late Late Show was doing precisely what those in authority thought that television should not do. What those in authority did not understand, and what Gay Byrne lived for, was the logic of a good show, the fact that fireside chats and the masterpieces of architecture put the plain people of Ireland to sleep, while brawls and revelations kept them up and watching.

The authorities - the bishops, politicians, county councillors, GAA officials, Vocational Educational Committees - realised very

169

quickly what was afoot, but they had great difficulty in doing anything about it. It is significant that of all the avalanche of protests that began in 1966 when a hapless woman called Eileen Fox revealed on the show that she had worn nothing on the night of her honeymoon and continued when Brian Trevaskis called the Bishop of Galway a moron, very little was directed at Gay Byrne personally. The objects of attack were television in general, the Late Late Show, RTE.

The show could be described by Loughrea Town Commissioners as "a dirty programme that should be abolished altogether", or criticised by Meath VEC for its "mediocrity, anti-national tone and recently low moral tone", but the objectors knew better than to accuse Gay Byrne himself of being dirty or morally low and were thus left flailing at abstractions. Gay Byrne's personality was crucial in that he became an Irish Everyman, spanning the past and the present, the traditional and the modern. Neat, sober and kind to old ladies, he was the son every Irish mammy would like to have had. Suave, brash and upwardly mobile, he was the man every mother's son dragging himself up by his bootstraps would like to be.

Only two aspects of Gay Byrne's personality (as opposed to his professional skills) are important to his broadcasting achievement, but both are essential to the survival of his shows. The first is that his own life represents in microcosm much of what has happened to Ireland in the past 30 years. Brought up in a sheltered, frugal and conservative family environment. Inculcated by the Christian Brothers with the values of piety, hard work and patriotism. Emigrating to England along with everyone else in the 1950s. Coming back along with everyone else in the 1960s. Getting richer as the country gets richer. Suffering financial calamity in the 1980s and contemplating emigration again.

His personal odyssey, then, has followed the same course as the national epic, the same serpentine currents of hope and despair, of excitement and boredom. Because he had been shaped by those conflicting currents, he can be compared by one person to the leader of godless Communism, by another to a Christian Brother. Senator J.B. Quigley saw him as Stalin: "Like Khrushchev, I am all against the cult of the personality." June Levine saw him as often "like a Christian Brother of the nasty type Irishmen have described to me, merciless, unreasonable, relentless in his attack on anyone who fell short." What he is most like, though, is contemporary Ireland - fluid, contradictory, elusive, a country in which the terms either/or

170

are replaced by the terms both/and. Gay Byrne, like his country is both traditional and modern, both conservative and liberal, both Catholic and materialist. The relative emptiness of his public persona is his greatest strength, keeping him from freezing in any set of unified attitudes, keeping him close to the irregular pulse of Irish life.

The other aspect of his personality that is important is related to this emptiness: the fact that he is, at heart, an actor. From a very early age, he wanted to act, and it was in the drama academies and the Dublin Shakespeare Society that he created himself as a performer. It is very doubtful if he would have had the emotional commitment, the imaginative sympathy, to be a really good actor, but it is the playing of roles which still keeps him going. On the one hand, there are the funny voices, the prancing around the studio with a contraceptive cap on his head, the willingness to have darts thrown at him or to have a melon on his chest chopped in half with a samurai sword. This aspect of his showing-off has preserved his shows as Light Entertainment, making the more serious and unpalatable parts of them just a part of the package in which the junkie with AIDS will be followed by a song and dance - after the commercial break.

The other side of the acting is the detachment, the coldness. He can ask the hurtful, nasty, embarrassing questions because it is in the script, because it is the role he is playing, because the interviewee is playing a part, too, and is not to be thought of as a bundle of real fears and emotions. R.D. Laing is drunk and crumbling in front of the cameras: confront him with his drunkenness and shuffle him off. E.P. Thompson, at the time the most influential intellectual in Europe as leader of European Nuclear Disarmament, is getting a bit complicated: cut him off after a few minutes, turn to the model from "Celebrity Squares" who was the previous guest and get her to talk about nuclear disarmament instead. Ask Des O' Malley about his meeting with Charles Haughey during the Arms Trial, ask Father Bernard Lynch if he's gay. Don't flinch, don't hedge, don't even change the tone of voice. How, the victims ask, can he be so nice one moment and so nasty the next? The answer is that neither the niceness nor the nastiness are anything personal, just a change of roles.

It is the slippery quality, this refusal to be fish of flesh, one thing or the other, that his enemies have always recognised as Gay Byrne's most dangerous quality. His one consistent credo, the one thing in his public persona which could be described as a principle

171

rather than an attitude, is that it is in the nature of television to throw everything in together, to refuse to recognise the distinctions between entertainment and seriousness, and that the medium, rather than any set of rules, has be to respected. "When the new toy called television came to Ireland," he recalled in an interview in the gay magazine OUT a few years ago "we had to recruit a whole new crop of people, young people, to come in and run it because the old school of radio did not know how to run this new thing, this new machine. Those new people had none of the ethics or ethos which would have been picked up in Radio Eireann and they saw no reason why we should not examine all the topics and the controversial issues and the things which affected people in real life, rather than the imaginary things that affected imaginary people."

This tendency to see television as something which makes its own rules as it goes along has been resisted from the start. The most consistent tack of those who find Gay Byrne uncomfortable is to demand, not that he be removed, but that he be defined: serious or entertaining? "Telefis," wrote the TV critic of the "Irish Catholic" in 1966 "has the responsibility to define which programmes are suitable for responsible expressions of views of important controversial content and which programmes by their nature are unsuitable for this... If the Late Late Show is to become a place for expression of views in which selected guests can say what they like, then it must be acknowledged and prepared as a serious discussion programme... There would have to be a chairman who preserves a balance rather than throw in innocuous comments or asides which amount to an uneasy handwashing...If, on the other hand, it is not intended to be such, but to be merely a form of entertainment, then it must be controlled so that nobody uses it, no matter how sincerely, for soap box oratory."

Sixteen years later, almost exactly the same argument was being made by Fred O'Donovan, then Chairman of the RTE Authority, when he banned a Late Late Show discussion on the abortion referendum. "Because of the emotional situation with cameras, people say things they wouldn't normally say. This is too important a subject to be treated trivally." The same things had happened before - in 1968, when the show was prevented from discussing a biography of Eamon de Valera on the grounds that it would be "inappropriate in the context of the Late Late Show" and again was prevented from broadcasting a programme on the defeat of the

Government in a referendum on proportional representation. The implicit message was always the same: if serious things were to be discussed, they should be discussed on serious, predictable programmes where the ground rules had been worked out in advance. Gay Byrne's openness and unpredictability were dangerous because people might "say things they wouldn't normally say".

Government ministers, particularly Fianna Fail ministers, have always been reluctant to be interviewed by Gay Byrne, not so much because they are afraid he will make them say things they'd rather not have said but because his whole style refuses to recognise them as fundamentally different from the knife-thrower or the film star. To submit to Gay Byrne is to submit to being treated as Entertainment, to being stripped of office, record, power, everything except your ability to hold the audience's attention for five minutes or 50 minutes. Pan Collins, the former Late Late Show researcher, once wrote that her job was "to produce a list of possible guests under six different headings: an intellectual, a glamour personality, a VIP, a cynic, a comic and a cookie character."

But in Gay Byrne's hands, the borderlines between those categories fall away. The intellectual of one shot can be made the cookie character of the next. The cynic who performs well can become a glamour personality in the space of a few minutes. The VIP who tries to be pompous ends up as the unintentional comic. Where a current affairs programme like "Today Tonight" treats people according to the category it finds them in - expert, economist, political leader, victim - the Late Late makes and unmakes the categories as it goes along treating people by their performance, not their past record. Gay Byrne, the man who made his way up in Irish society solely through his ability to entertain has always presented entertainment as uncomfortably egalitarian. Anyone can speak, so long as they speak entertainingly enough. Anything can be said, so long as it's gripping enough.

The late Archbishop Kevin McNamara probably had the Late Late Show and the Gay Byrne Show in mind when he bemoaned the loss of traditional authority in Irish society in 1985: "(There are) certain topics which have exercised the greatest minds for centuries, and on which a fund of traditional wisdom has been built up slowly and with difficulty over the years. These today are regarded as suitable topics for chat shows, on radio and TV, in which speakers of little or no qualifications parade with confidence the most varying and contradictory opinions..." He was, of course, right to be

173

concerned, for in Gay Byrne's pluralist republic of entertainment, the bishop owes his authority not to tradition but to his ability to sing an oul' song and the politician's power can be diminished by his inability to tell a good yarn.

Though not, of course, a yarn like this one:

Two days before Good Friday, in that year, it was potato-setting day. This was the 1940's and all the potatoes were still sown by hand, so everyone had to help, including Mary, who was heavily pregnant. Mary was the servant girl who worked 13 hours a day, cleaning, cooking, milking, feeding, who was 28 years old and a beautiful singer, who had made love to a man in a nearby village with nine children of his own. Just before dinner time, Mary rushed into the house to help with the serving. She had no dinner herself, complained of a blinding headache, and asked for an hour or two off to go to bed.

After an hour or so, Mary's employer called to her bedroom door. The door was locked but Mary called through it that she was much better and would be up shortly. After another hour, the house was filled with the screams of a new baby. The woman of the house got her husband, who went a few miles away and fetched Mary's elderly father. Mary still had the door locked and after they forced it down, she denied everything. They searched the room and found a little baby boy choked by a stocking, packed with her clothes in her suitcase. Mary's father walked her home and carried the case, in which later that night, the baby was buried. Mary went back to work two days later and that was the end of the matter. She got no help or care; "it didn't", the letter said "exist then".

We wouldn't know Mary's story without Gay Byrne, who included it on February 23rd, 1984, in the most devastating piece of broadcasting yet heard in Ireland: 50 almost uninterrupted minutes of letters unleashed by the death in childbirth of Anne Lovett in Granard. By then, Gay Byrne's centre of gravity had shifted from television to radio, from the dramatic to the confessional, just as the centre of national debate had moved from the public to the private. By then, a woman who did wear a nightie on her honeymoon would be the cookie character and soon the Leader of the Opposition rather than a Trinity student would be calling bishops names. The exposed nerves were now in more intimate and more painful places.

That programme let it all fly in a controlled but relentless onslaught of terrible intimacies. A sort of secret history of modern Ireland emerged that day with stories from every decade since the 1940s, stories that had been told to no one, stories that been bottled

174

up and swallowed down. There was only one person in Ireland to whom those stories could be told: someone who had been around long enough to become part of the national conscience, someone who had been pushing back, bit by imperceptible bit, the limits of what could be said in public, someone who was professionally unshockable, someone who was yet so unknown that his judgement or retribution need not be feared - Gay Byrne. It was to our shame that there was no one else to speak to, to our shame that we needed Gay Byrne so much. It was to his credit that he had survived long enough to be there when he was needed.

In the last of those letters, the writer concluded: "We did not wish to be nosy, but merely to share in their sorrow, as indeed we should." Much of the time over the past three decades, Gay Byrne has fed our nosiness and fed off it. But at his best he has helped us to share in the sorrow, as indeed we should. Perhaps, out of that sharing, there will come a day when we can hear our intimacies in a voice that doesn't come from the radio, can speak to each other in tones other than Gay Byrne's. On that day, if it comes, Gay Byrne will become what he hasn't been for 27 years: an ordinary broadcaster.

The Irish Times, September 1989.

DON'T BELIEVE A WORD

The life and death of Phil Lynott

Leighlin, Clonmacnoise, Ferns, Kells, Bangor, Lismore, Clogher. The centre of the corporation estate of Crumlin was started in the year of the Eucharistic Congress and built in the shape of the Eucharistic Cross. The roads were named after the dioceses of the Irish Catholic Church. Out here it was new territory, a kind of Ireland - suburban and working-class - not known before. As if to magic away the uncertainty of what might emerge from these winding rows of pebble-dashed two-up-and-two-downs, the planners gave them the shape and the names of the greatest institution of Irish tradition - the church. Happy homes and happy families, with the huge vaulted church and the granite barracks-like police station to look down and smile, and not a whisper of rock and roll on the distant breezes.

> *I'm a little black boy*
> *and I don't know my place,*
> *I'm just a little black boy*
> *I just threw my ace*
> *I'm a little black boy*
> *Recognise my face.*
> *(Phil Lynott, Black Boys on the Corner)*

Phil Lynott was born on 20 August 1951 and brought up on Leighlin Road, but his happy family was not the kind which the planners dreamed of. His father had never been around. He lived with his grandmother and his two uncles, Peter and Timmy. Timmy worked and kept the family going, not poor, just making ends meet. Granny was the matriarch. But Peter was the dreamer and Peter was the rocker. At Armagh Road CBS primary school, the topical taunt "Ya Baluba!" had an extra cutting edge when aimed at the little black boy, and Philip, though he suffered no serious racism, was more self-conscious, more angular, than the other kids. But with that self consciousness was a new reason to be proud.

The music that Uncle Peter listened to was soul and rhythm and blues, black music, even if it was sung by whites. Philip grew up with The Yardbirds, The Who, The Animals, led by his hero Eric Burdon, and, beyond that, with the black soul music of the STAX label singers. Later, when his uncle Peter turned down the job of singing with The Black Eagles, the first Crumlin rock band, Philip would take his place.

The music never completely filled the gap left by his father. Philip looked for heroes, in books and in the cinema. At the Roxy and the Stella he acquired a taste for stand up saviours, lone men pitted against the world. In his songs he would again and again return to the figure of the hero, of the Wild West or of Celtic mythology. Thinking of himself as an orphan, he had himself adopted by the heroic loners of his dream world. He called one of his first bands The Orphanage and wrote songs like "Shades Of a Blue Orphanage" ("...the Roxy and the Stella/where film stars starred/that's where me and Hopalong Cassidy, Roy Rodgers got drunk and jarred/and we might have been/the saviours of men/the captured captain in the devil's demon den.")

There were times, after he had grown up and become famous, when he went looking for his father. He looked in the big cities of the western world. He even ended up once in Rio, where his father might have come from. In the end, he invented myths about his father, writing him into cosy domestic scenes in his songs, or transporting him into the realm of the legendary heroes. In his 1973 Thin Lizzy album Vagabonds of the Western World he had a song, "Legend of the Vagabond", in which a mysterious traveller from afar meets and falls in love with a young girl, fathers a child by her and leaves on the night the child is born. "It is written from that day to this, all male descendants/Of the fatherless child are blessed in the art of love/to win the heart of any, but cursed never to be in love/or they will grow old and wither." Phil Lynott, the fatherless child, never grew old and withered. But he never stopped thinking of himself as an orphan.

> *Father and I waved goodbye*
> *As we went to look*
> *Uncle Peter was writing a book*
> *And his mama was starting to cook*
> *And she's ageing*
> *(Saga of the Ageing Orphan)*

Armagh Road primary school had no secondary school attached.

The boys from ambitious families, the ones anxious to take advantage of the new benefits of free education went on to Drimnagh Castle, a hub of the new meritocracy. The others went to Clogher Road Tech. Philip Lynott went to the Tech and stayed until he was fifteen. He went on to Tonge and Taggart metal works as an apprentice, going to Bolton Street College of Technology on day release to study mechanical drawing. Except for the music, it was a normal working-class upbringing. But the music was everything. Shortly after he left the Tech, Philip returned to play a gig in the school hall, making a big splash, putting on the style. He loved the idea of being king in a world where the teachers' writ didn't run, where you could make it big without them.

In the mid-sixties, Dublin had a bit of money, a lot of young people and a hunger for the new rock music. Music clubs, where bands played and the audience drank minerals, blossomed. There was the Club A Go-Go, the Five Club, the Moulin Rouge, the Flamingo, the Seventeen Club, the Scene Club, Club Arthur, the Apartment. The clubs were small and the entrance was cheap but there was enough work around to keep a succession of new bands going. The bands played the clubs on a four-week circuit, returning to the same place and pretty much the same audience every month. There were also gigs at tennis clubs outside the city centre, in Templeogue and Terenure, and halls in Fairview, Donnybrook, and Phibsboro.

Phil Lynott's first band, The Black Eagles, formed in Crumlin in 1968, with a line-up that would soon include the Thin Lizzy drummer Brian Downey, played in a few of the clubs while Downey and Lynott were still at Clogher Road Tech, as well as finding a place on the bill of the large rock concerts in Crumlin's Apollo cinema. By the time they left school, the band had split, but Philip had tasted the tang of rock and roll, and moved on to another local Crumlin band, Kama Sutra. In 1969 he became the singer with Brush Shiels' Skid Row.

Psychedelia hit Dublin in 1968, and Skid Row were its harbingers. The bands around the clubs until then, bands like The Vampires and The Strangers, still thought that "Good Vibrations" and "The Sloop John B." were far-out numbers. Skid Row brought echo chambers, liquid lights, and smoke bombs and Little Mick's eight millimetre films. Little Mick would film the band in one club and show the movie behind them while they played at the next one. Skid Row were louder, weirder and hipper than anyone had ever dared to be in Dublin before. Philip was getting into the I Ching,

178

Kafka, and acid before anyone else. He was listening to The Fugs and The Velvet Underground when hardly anyone else in Ireland had even heard of them. Philip, they said, was really sussed.

By the time Philip was pushed out of Skid Row - he had tonsillitis and Gary Moore could sing as well as playing lead guitar - he had learned a lot about style, about giving the people something different. He had also learned the peculiar mixture of an arty romanticism and macho hardman strutting that would become his image for stardom. By the time he formed Thin Lizzy in 1970 with Brian Downey and the Belfast duo of guitarist Eric Bell and keyboard player Eric Wrixon (Wrixon was let go half way through the band's first year and subsequently written out of the official biographies - the rock and roll business has no tears for the ones who don't make it) Philip had a persona to sell.

> *I am your main man if you're looking for trouble*
> *I'll take no lip 'cause no one's tougher than me.*
> *If I kicked your face you'd be seeing double,*
> *Hey little girl keep your hands off me.*
> *(The Rocker)*

Macho is an exaggerated masculinity in which an aggressive toughness goes easily with a romantic posture, and Philip, by the time he was twenty, had adopted the style. He didn't mind fighting but he liked a stylish fight, one hard punch and walk away. He took on the classic Latin macho image, growing a thin Latin moustache, and wearing toreador outfits, with short jackets coming to the waist, of his own invention. On him, they looked good and he earned extra money doing fashion spreads for women's magazines. In his songs he would refer often to Rudolph Valentino, and for Lizzy's follow up single to "Whiskey in the Jar", he released a classic Latin fantasy," Randolph's Tango", full of Latin moonlight and the boys at the ranch and a senorita looking pure as a dove, all in white. "Don't go my Randolph, slow tango with me."

As Thin Lizzy began to be successful, the macho confidence grew. Philip was the man who could handle anything, drink anyone under the table, get any women he wanted. One of the things he thought he could handle was drugs. In the early seventies in the Dublin rock scene, there was dope and acid. Smack (heroin) was a distant rumour; cocaine had hardly been heard of. That stuff would come later.

In 1970, Zhivago's night club opened in Dublin, a new kind of place where you drank alcohol instead of minerals while you danced the night away. The clubs, where the Dublin rock scene had blossomed, fell into sharp decline, and bands like Thin Lizzy were much too heavy for the more sophisticated night clubs, who preferred the control of discos to the wild frenzy of live rock. Lizzy were smart enough to see the change coming and moved out into the still-thriving ballrooms, building themselves a national following in the way that very few rock bands had done. There were "heads" in the country too, and Lizzy, six months into their career, got a run on the ABC ballroom circuit, playing a one hour set, sandwiched between the showband's two sets. For this they got £150 a night. In the Dublin clubs, they had been getting about £35.

Particularly after Eric Wrixon had been pushed out, and the band reduced to a three piece, the rock business began to provide a passable, if by no means decent, living. In Dublin there were still the larger ballrooms, the TV Club, the Crystal and Ierne, which could attract a crowd of up to eight hundred for their Teenage Friday Nights. In June 1970, Thin Lizzy did a one-off deal with EMI/Parlophone, who pressed a single "The Farmer". Even if it only sold 273 copies, it at least proved that they were a real rock band.

More importantly, they were an Irish rock band. Philip's black skin and lithe style had an exotic air and the band's thunderous sound was like nothing from the Ballroom of Romance, but his accent was unmistakable. In their early days Lizzy did Jimi Hendrix numbers and a loud, brash, twenty-minute version of "Dancing in the Streets", the sixties' hit recently re-released by David Bowie and Mick Jagger. The song lists the names of American cities, from Chicago to New Orleans. When Philip sang it, he shouted an extended litany of Irish towns, from Cork to Ballina, like a country and western singer singing the right song for the locality of the ballroom. If the harsh violent sounds of hard rock were a culture shock to the Irish, Thin Lizzy narrowed the gap and nationalised the music.

And everywhere the band went, there were women. For Philip the women were not just an occupational perk, they were in a real sense a part of the business. He had a woman every night and argued that it was good for the band's business. He brought the women to the gigs, the women brought the men. Sex was a personalised form of PR for the band, a way of building up a loyal following. The macho style became more than a style, it became a part of his way of life. Like the drugs, it was a habit he would never kick.

180

Don't believe me if I tell you
Not a word of this is true
Don't believe me if I tell you
Especially if I tell you that
I'm in love with you.
  (Don't Believe A Word)

London was the place to be for a young rock band, and to get there the band needed management. Their first manager, Terry O'Neill, sold his rights on Thin Lizzy for £150 to Pete Bardon and Brian Tuite, who had connections across the water. The band moved to London to heel up on Granny's Intentions, the band who, with Skid Row, had found the path for Irish acts into the big time and the big city. They signed up with Decca Records in November 1970 and five months later, released their first album, *Thin Lizzy*. But the money in London for live bands was considerably lower than the going rates in Ireland and until the beginning of 1973 when "Whiskey in the Jar" became a freak hit for the band, they survived in England only on the strength of twice yearly Irish tours. At this stage, the band could command £300 a night in the ballrooms of Ireland, which meant that they could make £6,000 in three weeks of hard slogging at home. After everything was paid for, there was enough to subsist in London for the rest of the year.

Even after the success of "Whiskey in the Jar", which reached number six in the British charts in February 1973, Phil Lynott wasn't rich. The money from the record was enough for a decent flat and better band equipment, but it wasn't until May 1976, when "The Boys Are Back in Town" made the top ten in Britain and America, taking the album *Jailbreak* with it, that Philip became rich. Within a month he was seriously ill with hepatitis, forcing the cancellation of the band's crucial American tour. From then until his death, he never broke down again, and even though he was using both heroin and cocaine, his high energy made him believe that he could take it on and beat it, like anything else. He had it sussed.

He had the music business sussed too. When the bloated old rock order was toppled by punk in 1977, Thin Lizzy survived. Philip helped Bob Geldof, about to sweep into the charts on the coat tails of punk, to get established in London. He turned up at all the wild parties for the young bands who were just about to make it big. He had the stamina to out-party them all. While the others were being written off as boring has-beens, Philip retained the confidence of the industry. He could still cut it in the wild man stakes. By the end

181

of 1978 he was playing with the *enfants terribles* of the new wave, The Sex Pistols, in a pick-up band called The Greedy Bastards, in both Dublin and London. While the others were retiring to their country mansions to play the family man, Philip was riding the new energy and taking care of the business. He had been doing it a lot longer than any of the young pretenders and he wasn't going to stop.

Bands on tour have contracts. There's the money, of course, by now around £20,000 for the services of Phil Lynott, but there's also the extras. The little bands get a crate of beer in the dressing room. Further up the scale it's beer, and a bottle of brandy, a bottle of tequila and a bottle of white wine, chilled. Thin Lizzy reached the heights where it could be six dozen bottles of German pils, a case of champagne, a bottle of the best cognac, and what's a few hundred quid on drink out of a gig that's costing £20,000?

Cocaine keeps you sober. It boosts your energy and keeps you from falling apart, even if you're drinking most of the night and getting out on the road again early the next morning. It also hides the debilitating effects of heroin. And it keeps you going in a world of lonesome heroes who take on the world and beat it. It's okay so long as you can handle it, so long as you have it sussed.

> *Now I've been messing with the heavy stuff*
> *And for a time I couldn't get enough*
> *But I'm waking up and it's wearing off.*
> *Junk don't take you far.*
> *Tell my mama I'm coming home*
> *And in my youth I'm getting older*
> *And I think it's lost control.*
> *Mama, I'm coming home*
> *Got to give it up*
> *Give it up*
> *Got to give it up, that stuff*
> *Got to give it up.*
> *(Got To Give It Up)*

On Sunday 5 January 1986, Heavy Metal Heather cashed in her chips. She told her story to "The Mirror" and for the next two days it ran under the banner "The Private Hell Of My Rock Hero". She wasn't called Heavy Metal Heather, which was the name she went by in the rock world, but "Heather Mitson, the housewife who shared the life of doomed rock star Phil Lynott." "Housewife

Heather Mitson had everything anyone could wish for - a loving husband, a pleasant home and all the comforts money can buy. But, like millions of other suburban housewives she dreamed and longed for the excitment and glamour that was missing in her respectable life." When Phil Lynott died, Heather got in first with her story of life with the tragic star. Dozens of other women could have told the same story, but Heather got in first and had two days of fame as his "ex-girlfriend". It was the last star turn for Phil Lynott, the final bow to the public for whom he had played at being a hero. "All I've done," Heather told "The Mirror" on the Monday after his death "is to write his epitaph."

> *Dear Lord take the time*
> *I believed your story now you believe mine*
> *Give me dignity*
> *Restore my sanity*
> *My vanity is killing me.*
> *(Dear Lord)*

(All lyrics quoted are from "A Collected Works of Philip Lynott", published in 1980.)

Magill, January, 1986.

HOME FROM HOME

The man, the judge felt, must be mad. He had walked into the GPO in Dublin, our greatest national shrine, and thrown a stone through a window. He had then gone into Middle Abbey Street and thrown another stone through another window, this time belonging to a trendy boutique. But it wasn't this which made the judge think him mad. It was the fact that he kept trying to insist on the magnitude of his crimes. When the arresting garda told the court that the boutique window was worth £50, the man interjected "It was worth more than that, it was a real, big expensive window." The man had earlier complained that sentencing policy wasn't what it used to be. Judges were being far too lenient. He was getting only short terms and what he wanted was a "decent sentence". The judge remanded him for psychiatric reports, saying that there must be something wrong with a person who wanted to stay in prison.

I haven't seen the psychiatric reports, but it would seem obvious that the man is perfectly sane. He is seventy one years old and homeless. The hard rain of an Irish winter has arrived, the damp and bitter winds that chill your bones to the very marrow are on their way. Worse, perhaps, Christmas is coming, with its hysterical happiness and gaudy gaiety pouring onto the streets, its imagery of log fires and mince pies and united families calculated to torment the homeless. Prison, at least, is warm, and it seems to me to be the height of sanity to prefer the status of honest outcast to the enforced bonhomie and fellow-feeling of the businessmen who once a year put on an apron and serve a Christmas dinner to the homeless, pretending that our society is one big happy family.

Far from being mad, the man's basic desire is for what we all recognise as the most normal of human things: home. "Prison," someone who knows him told me "is the place he knows as home. He knows the people, he knows the routine, he knows that he'll get a good meal and a bed." he man spent much of his life in the British Army and most of the rest of it in and out of prison, often being out for as little as a week at a time. Every time he gets out, he does something to get himself back in again. He has over a hundred

184

convictions to his credit. He has an old age pension and the community welfare people do their best for him. He stays at the Morning Star hostel when he's not in prison. But he doesn't know what to do with money: it is literally meaningless to him. "You can give him money" says a woman who has dealt with him "but the thing he's looking for is warmth. And the nearest thing he knows to warmth is prison."

"There are" she says "quite a number of older men like him. They talk about prison officers the way the rest of us talk about our families, calling them by their first names. It's all some of them have to talk about. Prison is the only place they feel safe and secure. Some of them want to get inside even to get away from the nonsense of Christmas. They get angry at Christmas, at the way people like them are used at Christmas time to make us all feel good." Prison, at least, is not sanctimonious about itself.

Who is mad and who is sane? The man who breaks the windows is referred to the psychiatrists because, in his world, prison is home. The sane world, meantime, acts with calculation and rationality. In another recent case in the Dublin courts, an old woman got an eviction order awarded against her. She had lived in a house in Clontarf for 19 years and ten months. Her landlord realised that if she made it 20 years, she would acquire rights, like the right to a 35-year lease. He decided to evict her and the court had no choice but to let him do so. If the woman had been a business, she would have acquired her rights to a lease after three years occupancy.

Nobody thought to refer the landlord to psychiatrists: he is patently an exemplar of rational behaviour in our society, a rationality measured out in figures and calculations and bottom lines. Homelessness throws up, indeed, lots of cold, hard figures. Eighty percent of people in private rented accomodation have no rent book and therefore not even the beginnings of enforceable statutory rights. You are entitled to a receipt if you buy a bar of chocolate, but not if you pay rent on the place you call home. The Department of the Environment is currently dithering about whether or not to introduce a legal right to a rent book. 70 per cent of people in private rented accomodation are on week-to-week tenancies, liable to be told to go at seven day's notice. The average time spent with a person who goes to Dublin Corporation's Homeless Persons Unit seeking assistance is two and a half minutes. Twenty five per cent of people who are housed by the same unit leave the places they are given within six months, because the housing is grossly unsuited to their needs. The number of houses being built by local authorities has declined drastically in the last three years. These are the rational, sane facts that lie behind the madness of the window-breakers.

As Eithne FitzGerald of the National Campaign for the Homeless points out, the country rose in revolt a hundred years ago over the 3 Fs: fair rent, free sale and fixity of tenure. But that was rural Ireland and the national struggle against the Saxon invader. The only F that operates for people who are dependent on the free market for a home is Free Sale: the freedom of the landlords to sell those homes out from under their tenants. The recent property boom has been a nightmare for vulnerable people in rented accomodation, who faced the demands of "vacant possession" or of increased rents.

Yesterday, lots of forms arrived at the headquarters of the Department of the Environment in Dublin. They are from local authorities around the country, fulfilling their requirement under Section 9 of the Housing Act to complete by 1 November their assessment of the numbers of homeless people in their area. Those who work with the homeless fear that the assessments will not tell the real story. In the Dublin Corporation area, for instance, the verbal guidelines being operated under instruction from the Department of the Environment are to include only those who could be housed in conventional accomodation. People like the window-breaker, people who can't be used to fill the vacancies on the housing lists created when the government offered £5000 to people to get out of local authority housing, creating new suburban ghettoes where anyone who could possibly leave has left, will not be on the list, will not figure even as statistics. If they can't be categorised as homeless, the next best thing is to get the psychiatrists to categorise them as mad.

Yesterday, the man who broke the windows was back in the Dublin District Court. He had been remanded in custody on a number of occasions while the court tried derperately to decide what to do with him. While rich prisoners hire good lawyers to get them off, he had sacked his lawyers, presumably in the hope that the worse his defence, the better his chance of getting a "decent sentence". He had intimated that, if they didn't send him down this time, he would have to go out and do something worse. The court, quite reasonably, was loathe to send him to prison at all: he is clearly not a dangerous criminal. And his problem is that even if he gets three months, he might get time off for good behaviour - he is, after all, a model prisoner - and still be out for Christmas. He would then have to look at us all, singing carols for the homeless.

The Irish Times, November 1989.

DETAIL TO SOME, DISASTER TO OTHERS

As you read this this morning, two different groups of people will be preparing to face into two very different ordeals. One group, hopeful and fretful, will be made up of junior civil servants, entering the second day of their internal competition for promotion. It will be an important day, for with cutbacks and embargos and hard-edged efficiencies, promotion in the Civil Service these days is tougher and rarer than it used to be. Some will be nervous, some cocksure, some just chancing their arms. But all will be thinking of a better future, of the next few months or the next few years, of buying a house, perhaps, or getting married, of maybe having a more interesting job to do or a somewhat higher status in the order of things. What they are doing today is, through a curious route and through no fault of theirs, connected to what the second group will be facing.

This other group will be trying not to think of the future. The future they will be trying not to think of is not the next few months or the next few years, but the next few days or even hours. By now, the money will have run out. The teabags will be on their second squeezing. The film of margarine on the yellow-pack bread will be transparently thin. The butts will be torn open for their entrails of tobacco and whatever is salvaged will be rerolled. The kids, in the next few days, will get a few extra wallops. The night shelters will be busy.

For these people and their families - 50,000 Dubliners and their dependents - today or yesterday should have been dole day. Except that last week, when they went to collect their dole, they were given this week's payment as well, and a printed slip explaining that "A Civil Service-wide internal competition for staff is being held on Wednesday 17th and Thursday 18th January. In order to avoid any delays which might arise for you because of reduced staff attendance on these days, you will not need to attend this office next week." It is many years since the Civil Service had such exams for promotion from its clerical officer grade to that of executive officer. Half of its staff in Dublin social welfare offices applied. It was an awkward situation.

The point about this little incident, which is a boring administrative detail to most of us and a minor disaster to 50,000 people and their families, is not that it is an example of uncaring bureaucracy, of the faceless pursuing the jobless. It is the opposite. The Department of Social Welfare says that it took the decision to make a double payment not lightly but after much careful consideration. It didn't want its clients to be inconvenienced, to suffer the irritation of long delays and the indignity of interminable queues. The whole thing was carefully planned to avoid inconvenience, rows, hassle.

And I'm sure this is true. Presumably, it takes time to organise a double week's payment for so many people. Authorisations have to be signed in triplicate, nods given, accounts taken, computers informed. Whoever thought about this did what bureaucrats often fail to do: think ahead to what's actually going to happen in a particular place at a particular time. And there is no reason to think that she or he wasn't motivated at least as much by humanity as by convenience.

It says so much about the gulf between those who depend and those who are depended on, between one side of the counter and the other, that this act of decency was taken by many people who claim the dole as an affront, even an assault. In the careful planning that went into the whole thing, nobody planned to tell the people who were actually getting the money, or the organisations that help to look after some of them. The first they heard of it was when they arrived at the hatch and were given their money and their explanatory slip of paper.

Many of these people, no doubt, went home, put half of the money away and carried on as normal. That is what the Department of Social Welfare expected them to do. But, and this is where the great gulf in understanding comes in, to do that when you are living from hand to mouth requires a heroic effort of will. If you have a regular wage and a bank account and predictable commitments, then planning how you spend your money over, say, a month is no big deal. But if you live in the state of deferred pleasures and accumulated debts that we call poverty, then keeping your hands off cash in hand for a week is a very big deal indeed. For those who have very strong wills, it is a form of torture which can be endured. For those who haven't, it is an invitation to forget that you are poor for a week, to live like the people in the ads, to have another pint, to buy that pair of shoes for your kid, to pay off a bit of the money you borrowed to get some toys for the Christmas.

To do any of these things, is to be irresponsible, to have no thought for the future. But not thinking about the future is precisely how you live if you're poor. And for those who are most dependent and most marginal, it is not merely the future but also the present that needs to be obliterated, by drink or drugs. A double week's dole is a double invitation to oblivion. In the last week, many people will have accepted that invitation, and those who work with them knew nothing of the double payment until they began to see its consequences. Even a warning might have helped.

The gulf between officialdom and those whom it is meant to serve was at its widest, though, in some employment exchanges last week, where as well as their double payment and their slip of paper explaining it, many men and women also got another document. It was a ticket entitling them to free entry to Funderland, a huge and hugely expensive fun fair in Dublin. Free entry means that you get into the fair without paying, not that you don't have to pay for the rides, the amusements and the sweets. If you have three or four kids and you bring them to Funderland, £20 won't go very far. So, as well as an extra week's dole money, these women were also given the means to spend it. If they accepted that invitation, they are paying for it this week.

It was an apt image of the world in which we live. We can all go to the fair, but only some of us can go on the rides without having to pay a price in misery. We can all go on the dodgems, but only some of us really crash. We can all go on the big slide, but only some of us really come back to earth with a bang at the bottom. And so long as we are divided like this, one man's humane solution will be another man's poison.

The Irish Times, January, 1990.

ACKNOWLEDGEMENTS

Almost all the work in this book is journalism, with all of the curtailments of space and deadlines that that implies and, I hope, at least some of the immediacy and directness. I have therefore made very little effort to change these pieces, except in minor ways of restoring the odd sentence cut from the original publication, correcting typographical errors, and either removing or briefly explaining topical references which have since become obscure. In order to avoid repetition, two pieces, those on country and western music and on bungalows in section B have been supplemented with material written for Martin Parr's book of photographs, "A Fair Day", which is also where the essay "Land Beyond the Waves" was first published. Two other pieces have non-journalistic origins. The Introduction is based on an essay written for the Douglas Hyde Gallery. The essay "Meanwhile Back at the Ranch" was written as a lecture for the Canadian Association for Irish Studies.

As journalism, these pieces are the result to one degree or another of a collective effort. That effort is first of all that of the many, many people who spoke to me for the articles, whether they are directly quoted or not. Their voices shape these words, and I am immensely grateful to them all. Secondly, the effort belongs to the many editors who commissioned and published these pieces. I would not be a journalist without the work of David McKenna in "In Dublin", and subsequently at "Magill" Colm Toibin was a guide and a touchstone. Vincent Browne provided stimulation, encouragement and the freedom to explore areas that went beyond the headlines in The Sunday Tribune. John Waters was enthusiastic and sympathetic in his time at "Magill". And, finally, Conor Brady, Liam MacAuley and my colleagues at the Irish Times have given me both a secure home and the liberty to say what I want to say, both of which I regard as a real privilege.